CONFESSIONS

OF THE HIRED SPATULA

One Camp Cook's Accounting Of Some Humor,
Recipes And Nonsense In The Hills

Deborah Lynne Carlton

Front cover: *Pilot Peak* by Deborah Lynne Carlton
                Oil on canvas, Private Collection
Back Cover: *Line Lake* by Deborah Lynne Carlton
                Oil on canvas, property of the artist

Recipes: Original recipes by the author are indicated with (dc) in the Contents listing. Of the remaining recipes, some were obtained through on-line sources, sharing or good old swapping. Credit is given where origin is known.

These stories are mostly from my personal experiences, and I have taken the liberty to change names, where appropriate, in order to protect the privacy of others, as well as the continued wellbeing of myself. I reserve the right to claim any portion of this as fiction according to my moods, and quite frankly sometimes I have wished it was. Not everyone likes to be lampooned, but many warrant it, including myself. In particular, Shamus Henry is a fictitious name and you will not find him listed in any outfitter directory. Darby Mountain Outfitters, Coulter Lake Guest Ranch, The Flying B and The Root Ranch, etc. are true names and locations, in case you wish to make inquiry as a potential guest, however, the names of certain individuals within these stories have been altered. In general, none of these characters are terribly unique to the West - you could encounter them most anywhere if you keep a look out. Please do keep a look out.

National Library of Canada Cataloguing in Publication Data

Carlton, Deborah Lynne.
   Confessions of the hired spatula

ISBN 1-55212-748-6
1. Outdoor cookery. 2. Outdoor life--Humor. I. Title.
TX823.C37 2001   641.5'782   C2001
910675-0

TRAFFORD

This book was published *on-demand* in cooperation with Trafford Publishing.
On-demand publishing is a unique process and service of making a book available for retail sale to the public taking advantage of on-demand manufacturing and Internet marketing.
On-demand publishing includes promotions, retail sales, manufacturing, order fulfilment, accounting and collecting royalties on behalf of the author.

Suite 6E, 2333 Government St., Victoria, B.C. V8T 4P4, CANADA
Phone   250-383-6864   Toll-free   1-888-232-4444 (Canada & US)
Fax   250-383-6804   E-mail   sales@trafford.com
Web site   www.trafford.com   TRAFFORD PUBLISHING IS A DIVISION OF TRAFFORD HOLDINGS LTD.
Trafford Catalogue #01-0148   www.trafford.com/robots/01-0148.html

10   9   8   7   6   5   4   3

Books by Deborah Lynne Carlton

Confessions of the Hired Spatula
Lake Solitude

To my loving parents, with gratitude
and tranquilizers.

"Wyoming, where the men are men,
and the women are too"

TABLE OF CONTENTS

But First, A Few Relevant Terms ...

Chapter I – The Legend of Darby Mountain

Introduction
~   Quick Outfitter Beans
A Little Background
~   Fabulous Chocolate Chip Cookies*
Ivan the Terrible
~   Graduation Stew (Sausage Potato & Onion Stew) (dc)
~   Beer Bread
The Big Spender
~   Old South Peach Cobbler*
~   Caramel Sauce
How to Catch a Polar Bear
~   Fancy Polar Peas*
~   Bodacious Roasted Potatoes (dc)
Make His a Mule
~   Mule Butter (dc)
Pornographic Row
~   Spicy Lamb Chili*
Sunken Ship Springs
~   Saucy Cowboy Dip
~   Skinny Dip
Cookie Turns Into A Pumpkin
~   Honey Pumpkin Pie
~   Pumpkin Bread*
Payback
~   Butterfingers
Wimp and Bud
~   Hunter's Stew (dc)
~   Cheese Soup*
~   Wisconsin Cheddar Bacon Puffs*

The Couch Killer
- ~ Russ's Favorite Shotgun Turkey (dc)
- ~ Sweet Apple Stuffing & Gravy (dc)
- ~ Shotgun Turkey Soup (dc)
- ~ Sandra's Egg Noodles*
- ~ Shotgun Turkey Salad Sandwiches (dc)
- ~ Shotgun Turkey Pot Pie (dc)

The Watermelon Crawl
- ~ Chuck's Favorite Oatmeal (dc)
- ~ Fruit Compote (dc)

Rock Chickens
- ~ Perfect Rock Chicken (dc)

Moonlight Escapades at the Spring
- ~ Elk Pepper Steak*

Cookie Bags a Deer
- ~ LBJ's Favorite Venison Chili*
- ~ Venison Summer Sausage*

A Little Local Color
- ~ Pecos "Red" Stew*
- ~ Chili Cheese Cornbread

Heart Rocks
- ~ Grandma Beck's Sponge Cake*

<u>Chapter II – The Mystery of Coulter Lake</u>

My Brief Fling with Coulter Lake
- ~ Chili Cheese Omelet*
- ~ Orgasmic Cinnamon Rolls*

Yoo Hoo
- ~ Lord Charley's Corn Chowder*

Snowmobiling Fun With Skeeter
- ~ Chili Colorado*
- ~ Traditional Cornbread

Chapter III – The Misery Of Shamus Henry

The Night the Horses Run Off
~ Shoo Fly Cake
A Little Off-Trail Humor
~ Bear Shit*
Danged If They Didn't Run Off Again
~ Western Scrambled Eggs (dc)
~ Hash Browns (dc)
~ And Fresh Salsa on the Side
The World Famous Gil Hoss
~ Coon Pate'
Wulfie the Wonder Mule
~ Mule Biscuits*
The Star Wrangler
~ Prime Rib*
~ Golden Dinner Rolls*
Diamond Dave
~ Quick Chicken Southwest
The Florida Suite
~ Parrillada de Pollo "Florida" al Jugo Citrico*
~ Cuban Black Bean Soup
Lonesome Dove
~ Dove Dumplings*
~ Snickerdoodles* (cookies)
Cowboy Wannabes
~ Wannabeans*

Chapter IV – The Hell of the Root Ranch

The Flying Resorts
~ Flying Ferdinand's Marinated Roast*
The Gas Man
~ Ma's Apple Crisp or Stuffed Apples*
The Girls
~ Tossed Greens with Mandarin*

Captain Blowhard
~ Jerk Chicken*
Will: The Other White Meat
~ Roast Pork*
~ Honey Barbequed Ribs (dc)
~ Ma's BLT Potato Salad*

Chapter V — Moose Stories and Other Nonsense

Moosey Does The Watoosey
Parting of the Waters
The Great Moose Drive
~ Fiesta Moose Turd Balls*
Large And In Charge
The Devil Moose
Outfitter Update

Chapter VI — Exploring the West

Exploring The West
~ Trout in Foil
Campfire Cooking In General
~ Cowboy Coffee
An Excellent Camp Secret
What Is An Outfitter?
And Where Do I Find One?
State Outfitter Associations
~ Flea & Tick Spray

Chapter VII — Epilogue: Lessons That Linger

Summer of 2000
~ Rocky Mountain Oysters
~ Beer Batter

BUT FIRST, A FEW RELEVANT TERMS

ass-chewin'	inevitable result of major screw-up.; akin to getting ear bent, butt kicked or balled out.
bear wipe tree	just like it sounds, small trees that bears back up against and wipe/itch their butts, leaving distinct residue which remains long after offending incident.
beaver fever	giardia.
bell mare	lead mare, the one the herd is most likely to follow... for that reason a bell is placed on her neck at night.
bubbified	my own term for redneck, backcountry bubba.... "he's right bubbified"....
camp cash	anything in short supply, most notably TP or chew, which suddenly reaps inherent value.
camp jack	see definition of schlep.
change of mind	what happens to a male cow or horse after castration; focus changes from "ass to grass" as old cowboy Verne Johnson was known to say, may he rest in peace.
chaps	full length leather leggings worn for protection while riding or wrangling.
chesticles	the female version of testicles
chinks	shorter, calf-length version of chaps.
chinking	act of packing panniers with newspaper to prevent contents from rattling.
class I grizzly area	wilderness area designated as primary grizzly habitat; governed by strict food and storage restrictions.

cookie	generallly refers to anyone fool enough to sport an apron in the hills; in this case – ME.
cowboy carwash	who'd have known that little window washing tool at the gas station could be so handy?
cowboy foreplay	"shut up bitch and git in the truck!"
cowboy up	buck up; toughen up; quitcherwhinin'; the first and most essential of cowboy wannabe lingo.
cow poke	actual definition uncertain; always meant to ask origin of "cow … poke" though suspect it ain't polite.
crack house	place of business in Big Piney, Wyoming where proprietors are reputed to be large, and in need of suspenders.
crick	creek, stream or brook.
dead sea	Fontenelle Reservoir, where naught but carp and junk fish may thrive.
decked	dressed out, slugged, popped, cold cocked, smacked hard up side the head, etc.
designated wilderness area	remote area designated by government, managed by strict laws forbidding any form of wheeled or motor-ized transport (including bicycles) or assistance, including generators, chain saws, etc
drop pack	service offered by some outfitters whereby you are packed into a wilderness location, with planned provi-sion drops or pack out as you designate. Usually a rea sonable fee for this service.
dude	greenhorn, flatlander, anyone who ain't local or familiar with life in the hills; this would also be me.

fess up	spill the beans, tell the truth; derivative of confess.
fire on the mountain	heartburn, often followed but not limited to the trots, which can be tragic if you're traveling by horse.
five letter prince	prick (contributed by Sir John Powers).
fools hen	blue grouse, foolish fat mountain bird which don't know enough to run; also known as the dreaded rock chicken.
fuh' hellsake!	cowboy exclamation of dismay.
gaw	another cowboy exclamation of dismay; "**GAW** Cookie.... whatcha' do that for?
glassin'	spying, scoping, peeping on just about anything with binoculars, usually in reference to scouting game .
greenhorn	see definition of "dude."
halfbreeds	mules; reference alludes to mixed horse and donkey parentage of said mule.
hatchet knot	any knot requiring a hatchet to undo it.
hellbitch	particularly moody female horse; term sometimes applied to women at certain times of the month…
hobbles	leather shackles placed on a horse or mule's front legs, to restrict long distance travel; used during grazing.
horsin'	term for female horse in heat; "holy cow Ned, that filly's a horsin' – quick, lets get'er in the chute!"
ivories	two unique incisor teeth found only of the North American Elk; said to be this continent's only ivory-bearing mammal; often used in Native American women's costume; considered a trophy to elk hunters.

might could	regional prefix for pursuing an idea…"I might could help ya get that wood in tha' truck."
might not	what happens when greenhorns make fun of "might could."
mulies	Mule Deer, indigent deer species of the Western US.
open	livestock breeding term for "not pregnant," thereby "open" for a dose of bull.
orangutan	anything wild or unpredictable; such as a horse, a woman, or a tricky part of the back country.
orangu-tang	also a little known but popular cowboy cocktail consisting of Tang and whisky; credited to one John Fellow who actually drinks the stuff!
outfit	truck, rig, gear, set up; "say, that's a nice outfit ya got there … how many miles ya' got on her? not polite to ask about a man's woman, however.
outfitter	why the fellow what owns the outfit of course; also refers to a person or operation, which may be hired to pack you and your belongings into the hills, or guide a big game hunt.
pack string	multiple pack animals hitched together with rope.
panniers	evenly weighted packs which fit onto both sides of the pack saddle; used for hauling grub and supplies.
picking up the pieces	what the last person at the rear of the packstring does; generally means keeping an eye on pack animals and riders, alerting others to potential problems, and coming along behind to pick up the pieces; I would add my own version, which is "<u>inhaling</u> all the pieces." if you ever ride at the back, you will get my point..

pigging string	specially-tied ropes which bind pack animals together; wise men keep their thumbs clear of pigging strings…
pms	pretty much smoke (referring to fire); refer also to "hellbitch"
progressive trip	a moving pack trip where a minimal camp is set up at a new location every night or second night. good opportunity to see a lot of back country.
quakies	Quaking Aspens, common hardwood of the Western United States.
rag horn	young bull elk, maybe 2-3 years in age.
reefer	abandoned refrigerator semi-trailer, often used by outfitters to store equipment; not to be smoked.
red neck	see bubbified; more widely known term for men with red necks; blue collar or out of doors professions.
rock springers	hunters from Rock Springs, Wyoming; disliked by locals for their habit of hunting in Big Piney territory. "just never know about them "rock springers"…
rocky mountain oysters	western delicacy of specially prepared bull balls – COWBOY UP! (recipe contained herein).
shit happens in the woods	boony equivalent to "shit happens," only much more interesting.
schlepping	a schlep is one who does the grunt work; the act of which is called "schlepping."
sign	another aspect of shit happens in the woods; evidence of animal presence used in tracking.
spike	younger bull elk, maybe one year old.

spike camp	temporary hunt camp, usually consisting of small canvas tent, wood stove and sparse provisions compared to base camp.
sum a'bitch	most anything that confounds a man (I will keep it brief) instilling the desire to cuss, condemn or whup, respectively.
swamping	the act of bogging down vehicle in mud hole.
testicle festival	event in Missoula, Montana honoring and serving rocky mountain oysters; motto: "have a ball."
tits up	expired.
trots	the rear version of "fire on the mountain."
vegetarian	lousy hunter.
wapiti	native term for deer.
watermelon crawl	popular country song about the consequences of over-indulging on spiked watermelon; some outfitters have been known to observe this mode of travel on wintry nights.
worrush	Coloradan Redneck for "wash."
wrangle	handle horses.
wrangler	handler of horses.
wreck	accident of any kind, including but not limited to horses, pack strings and trucks.

CHAPTER I

The Legend of Darby Mountain

INTRODUCTION

What happens when an Eastern woman develops a great longing to explore the great outdoors, and that longing becomes too great to ignore?

Exactly the question I was asking myself not so long ago. Frustrated with my urban life and convinced there was a place where people could still live AND make a living out of doors, I set about to find it. That search led me to become a camp cook for outfitters and guest ranches for a while. Long enough to answer the question, and short enough to smarten up.

The year was 1993 and I was a burnt out legal secretary working for a semi-kamikaze attorney who apparently found venting stress on moi infinitely more satisfying than a worry stone. At this point, I was barely surviving each day at the office. Eyes glazed over and fixed on the distant horizon out my window – you might say I misplaced my sanity, and so it would follow that I had to go looking for it. There I was, discarding that East coast life and driving off into the great Western unknown. I didn't know what the place would look like, but I imagined there would be no computers, no telephones, and no LAWYERS. I was correct on at least two counts.

> Q: "Why do they bury lawyers 10 feet deep?
> A: 'Cause deep down, they're really nice guys."

Of course, getting to the West was the easy part. Finding that first job was not so simple. I had not heard of an "outfitter" before setting foot in Wyoming, never mind what cooking for one might entail. I had seen Western movies where crotchety old men like Slim Pickins slung hash, were respectfully called "Cookie" and, being as ornery as rattlesnakes, were seldom crossed. Naturally, I never pictured myself in Slim's shoes, and definitely not in that outfit, though I can now speculate as to why Slim was so ornery.

But as the chipmunks and the wild things were my witness, I did tell the man I would sure love to learn the trade, and I would work extra hard to make up for my extensive inexperience. I could cook, make things taste pretty good, and passably ride a horse. Throw in a superior sense of humor and some common sense and I expected I would survive all right. Besides which, I had to be better than the alternative, which was NOTHING. Basically, the man was desperate.

So that is how I found myself in a tent, in the hills, in Wyoming with nowhere to go but up. It was a pretty heady experience until it dawned on me just how much I had to learn. What I knew might have filled a cowboy hat. What I did NOT know could have easily filled Yellowstone Lake — well that is how it felt anyway.

Yes, the proverbial "hill of beans" is what I had to offer at that point, so we'll put BEANS on the menu and get to work!

QUICK OUTFITTER BEANS

Perfect for that first night in camp after a long pack trip!

1 lb.	hamburger
1 sm.	onion, chopped
¼ C.	catsup
¼ C.	BBQ sauce
1/3 C.	white sugar
1/3 C.	brown sugar
2 T.	molasses
1 T.	chili powder
1 tsp.	salt
1 tsp.	pepper
2 T.	mustard
1 can	pork 'n beans
1 can	butter beans
1 can	kidney beans
1 can	pinto beans
½ lb.	bacon, cooked and crumbled

Cook hamburger until brown. Add onion and cook until tender. Add remaining ingredients, except bacon. Put in Dutch oven and top with bacon crumbs and bake at 350°F degrees for an hour.

Can be cooked in crock-pot. Heat on high for an hour...reduce heat and cook 2-3 hours on medium heat.

A LITTLE BACKGROUND

With this small bit of foundation in place, allow me to jump ahead to the first hunting season just as a hunter arrived for his scheduled moose hunt. Since my outfitter boss, Chuck, was momentarily detained, I greeted the hunter and ushered him in. The hunter quickly assumed I was Mrs. Chuck, and it was not long before I heard myself being referred to as such. *"WHOA now, I am "the hired spatula" and nothing else in the way of relations to anybody... including any funny stuff."* If you don't set things straight, some people will assume all kinds of things -- and THEN some.

Chuck laughed nervously like he was worried I would scare the guy off, and the hunter was duly apologetic, especially since he had been fixing to compliment Chuck on his <u>nice</u> <u>young</u> "<u>Wahf</u>" (like I was a prized steer or something). Then the hunter exclaimed in mock horror, *"Oh NO Chuck, I have READ about these things, but I have never been around to see it happen — she is gonna run off with an elk hunter. She will leave you stranded right in the middle of hunt season. Can't have no single women around camp, yep she is gonna do it Chuck!"* He was having way too much fun with this.

> <u>Mental Note</u>: Feed that man lots of oatmeal — and maybe some tofu.

While life is a wondrous and uncertain thing, and though I am often curious of what fortune lies ahead, I can assure you, I never ran off with no elk hunter.

It is important to note that I did sport the name "Cookie" for the duration of this particular job, mainly because it was a camp tradition and it vexed them to change their ways. Guessing as much, I accepted the title. However, the daily dose of teasing from this bunch marked open season on all of them. I visualized an imaginary red bulls-eye on the back of every one of their heads, which, I mused, would come in handy during snowball season.

I began recording stories in my daily journal, mainly as a way of holding on to them. Years later, I realize there is no better way to put the past in perspective than to lampoon the hell out of everybody — including myself. Please forgive my bit of fun here. I hope you laugh as much as I do, though admittedly, I have often been accused of being the only one laughing at my own jokes.

Also, please know that while I may poke fun, I do not wish to depict the characters as idiots or buffoons. (However, if you come to that conclusion yourself, it cannot be helped.) Chuck's gang is a hard-working bunch of folks who know a lot more about being in the woods than I ever will. You could not hope for a better outfit to show you the rare beauty of the mountains and all its special places.

Shortly before that hunter departed, we had a nice chat where he ventured to comment that I did not fit the kind of woman he expected to find out here. I agreed, mainly because I was not <u>from</u> here (surprise). "Here" being Big Piney, Wyoming, population around 500, not counting the groundhogs. The hunter said he was a hard working miner and rancher from Utah, a "good Mormon" who had married a woman who'd be sure to keep up the house, have a hot meal waiting each night and make a fitting mother to his children. He admitted he did not so much love as appreciate her – and besides, she made superb beef jerky, both traditional and teriyaki flavored.

The hunter was right — I did not quite belong here, not socially anyway. But I loved the country and I managed a fair imitation of a cook so they put up with me, more or less. It was either that or starve.

Several years later, some old geezer piped up and queried, "*how come a purty thang like you ain't married?* I said it was because I was smarter than that, and I knew when to run.

FABULOUS CHOCOLATE CHIP COOKIES*

It seems fitting that one of the first recipes should be one of "Cookies." LOTS of cookies. So here it is, a fabulous all time favorite chocolate chip cookie recipe, in gargantuan proportions that defy the hips.

1x		4x	6x
¾ C	Butter Crisco	3 C.	4½ C.
1¼ C	brown sugar	3¾ C	6¼ C.
2 T.	milk	8 T.	12 T.
1 T.	vanilla	4 T.	6 T.
1	egg	4	6
1¾ C.	flour	7 C	10½ C.
1 tsp.	salt	4 tsp.	6 tsp.
¾ tsp.	baking soda	3 tsp.	4½ tsp.
1 C.	chocolate chips	4 C.	6 C.

Combine Crisco, brown sugar, milk, vanilla & eggs and mix well. In a separate bowl, mix dry ingredients, and then add in small amounts. Fork in chocolate chips and spoon out dollops on cookie sheets. Bake at 375°F for 8-10 minutes. Remove before they begin to brown.

*Basic recipe from, you guessed it, Crisco!

IVAN THE TERRIBLE

It's a common occurrence, and any outfitter can attest to the fact that shit happens in the woods. And so it came to pass that Chuck Thornton of Darby Mountain Outfitters found himself suddenly stranded in mid-season with neither cook nor wrangler. <u>Lesson One</u>: Never hire a husband and wife team. They up and quit him one day, leaving Chuck in a bit of a pickle. So Chuck put the word out for a new cook and prayed for help to arrive. <u>Lesson Two</u>: Be careful what you ask for.

Meanwhile, I had been camping several hundred miles away along the Wood River outside of Meeteetsie, Wyoming for nearly a month – hiking, swimming in the river, making landscape paintings of this lovely paradise and generally enjoying myself (when I wasn't worrying about money). In talking with locals and asking a lot of questions, I learned of this thing called "outfitter" and subsequently placed notice in the local bulletin.

Chuck's brother Monty, the local brand inspector, had seen my notice and no doubt heard some local scuttlebutt about that "fool artist woman driving around in a VOLKSwagon." After learning of Chuck's dilemma, Monty drove 30 miles out to my humble campsite at Brown Mountain to track me down. I might not have looked the part, but I was certainly anxious enough, and I had a pulse. So that is how I got my first cooking job – mutual desperation. Now to return to the story at hand.

Chuck's brother Ivan provided the first introduction to the world of camp cooking. Ivan had grudgingly donned the apron under protest and only until a replacement could be found. A retired Forestry Department man, Ivan was an old hand at being in the hills since he had been there all his life. Thus, it was his dubious honor to show the greenhorn the ropes. For sure, there are many tricks and bits of wisdom to camp cooking, and Ivan had a vested interest in compressing them all into one little pill for me to swallow so *to get himself out of the kitchen!* I have always hated pills. And Ivan was a fussy sort of thing (worry wart) with a fearsome set of teeth. I had nightmares about those teeth lest he should ever get upset with me. Cujo came to mind.

One day Ivan finally decided to join the daily trail ride (goody) and left me to tend camp. Mounting his favorite horse "Pinky" with a cocky swagger and a tip of his hat (be still my heart) Ivan departed with an air of authority. I did fantasize briefly of slipping a burr under his saddle, but at least I was alone and I relished the chance to enjoy some peace without ole' Fussbudget around. First off, I dispensed with Ivan's conservative menu and whipped up a sumptuous stew of sausage, peppers, onions and potatoes with a few spices tossed in, leaving it to simmer 'til thick and tender. That evening, Ivan lifted the lid, took one whiff, and solemnly pronounced me COOK, thereby removing himself from the kitchen ever after —

At some point, Ivan got talking about how he liked to go dancin.' And, apparently feeling frisky, decided to clue me in on his three most favorite things ... the first two were "dancin' and drinkin'."The third one was insinuated with a quick knowing wink, which made me blush. I did not fancy him the drinking type, but the thought of those clodhopper boots dancin' their way under my bed was not very appealing. I tactfully avoided the subject. Following dinner that evening, Ivan skipped the last course and headed to the bath tent for a good hot soak. This, being one of the coveted luxuries of the camp, a product of pure cowboy ingenuity in action. Water piped from a mountain spring high above camp, run into a steel drum, heated with firewood, and then run into the tub. (Caution: Check temperature before submersion. YeoOW!) Meanwhile, as I served dessert to the guests, Chuck smirked and pointedly suggested *"Maybe I'd like to bring Ivan's desert to him in the bath tent?*

*"NOPE, I think he'd like that just a little too **MUCH!**"*

It was hours before Ivan reappeared — plenty of time to begin worrying that Chuck told him what I had said — possibly embellishing it with a little brotherly spice. After all, they were kin! I grew hotly embarrassed and most fervently hoped to weasel out of an awkward scene — maybe avoid Ivan entirely! But eventually his big self loomed into the kitchen, confronting me with a kind of murderous look, clutching a fist and sputtering "**YoooOU**…" I was looking for possible escape routes in case things got ugly, but that was all. No cussing. No gnashing teeth. I live to cook again.

I never really knew what Chuck might have said to Ivan, if anything. Or what Ivan might have thought of me… if anything. But there was no further mention of Ivan's three favorite things.

And Ivan never did get dessert.

MOOSE IN REPOSE

MOOSE IN SPACE!

One day Ivan shared a little bit of comedy from his wilderness experiences. He'd been working through the mountains all day; at the end of which both he and the horse were pretty well beat. Heads hung low and plodding towards home, they came upon a cow moose that was so engrossed in preening herself that she failed to notice the onlookers. Ms. Moose was bedded down with her head all twisted around like a big moose pretzel, accessing those hard to reach spots on her back.

Ivan, possessing something of a sadistic humor could not resist unleashing a thundering war whoop, which nearly caused his immediate unseating from the startled horse. But the resulting spectacle of Ms. Moose was well worth it. Ivan scared the b'jezus out of her, sent her sprawling with all four legs up in the air. When she finally got collected she hightailed it down the trail, peeing all the way

Guess you could say he scared the piss out of her — literally.

GRADUATION STEW
(Sausage, Potato & Onion Stew)

My first original concoction as camp cook.

1-2 lbs	ground pork
1 clove	garlic, crushed, minced or powdered
1 lg.	onion, chopped in chunks
¼	green pepper, chopped fine
4	green onions with tops, chopped (optional)
3	potatoes, 1" cubed
1	beer, any brand
1-2 tsp.	thyme
1 tsp.	fennel seed
½ tsp.	black pepper
	soy sauce or salt to taste
	(save this step for last when stew is fully cooked)

Brown pork, drain to remove fat then set aside.

Sauté garlic, onion, pepper, etc., on medium/high heat until onions are clear. Add potatoes and pork, beer and water to cover (amount depending upon desired thickness), then bring to boil.

Reduce heat. Add spices, more or less to taste. Simmer until potatoes are tender. Adjust spicing and salt or soy sauce to taste.

<u>Serving Suggestions:</u> For variation, try adding fresh, canned corn or yellow hominy. Substitute pork for spicy Italian sausage. Stew goes great with Beer Bread.

BEER BREAD

This recipe was a staple in the Coulter Lake Guest Ranch kitchen. It is quick and painless to make, so long as you are not inclined to cry over spilt beer, and invariably, there are no leftovers.

3 C.	flour (unbleached)
½ C.	sugar
4 tsp.	baking powder
1 tsp.	salt

1	12 oz. beer (room temperature), alcohol or non-alcohol

Combine dry ingredients well in bowl, fork in beer just until ingredients moistened. Do not over stir!

Bake at 325°F for 55 minutes until top golden brown. Coat with butter and set to cool on rack.

For flavor variations:

- try ¼ tsp. of both dill weed and thyme mixed into dry ingredients.
- use half whole wheat flour to half regular unbleached flour.
- use dark ale or other variations of beer.
- substitute brown sugar or honey for table sugar.

THE BIG SPENDER

Archie is a true son of the South, though a piece of his heart (if not his pride) must surely lie somewhere in the West. Many times he has returned to Darby Mountain Outfitters, along with friends Les and Corky and their children for a father/child retreat.

I cooked for these folks only once. In fact, they were my first victims (or I was theirs) so I was quite anxious to make a good impression. But with this bunch it was not long before I relaxed, and I missed them dearly when they left.

This is one story told of summers past, recounted by Chuck well after Archie's Gang had departed. He knew better than to tell me when Archie was still around because I would surely have teased him. As I recall the story, Archie arrived one year with his latest prize perched square upon his head. A fancy hat he called the "Big Spender." Add a nice big stogie, substantial pistol at the hip, pose him on a horse with that smug Southern boy smile, and you get the picture. Archie was a piece of work.

One day Chuck took Archie's Gang riding up Mount Isabel (elev. 10,400), which features a fine view of the Grand Tetons over a hundred miles away. As a matter of tradition, Chuck lined everybody up under the ole "Hanging Tree" for a picture.

Just then you'd have thought Archie would be sitting up pretty. But there he was, fiddling with his fool Walkman, reins draped on the horse's neck, arms fully occupied with adjusting his headset, and don't look now, but the prized

Big Spender is perched on the saddle horn. It is not difficult to imagine how the wind came up just then, and how the Big Spender might go flying … and how a fella's horse might be wont to hop sideways from the dreaded hat monster. Indeed, that is just what happened. From Chuck's account, Archie's descent was like "a slow motion film segment in a John Wayne movie" complete with full belly landing which, I imagine, produced a sizeable cloud of dust. Wyoming is kind of dry that time of year. And whereas a person might normally be thankful for something to cushion his fall, Archie was FAR from thankful when he landed on top of the Big Spender. Yep, flattened it like a cow patty.

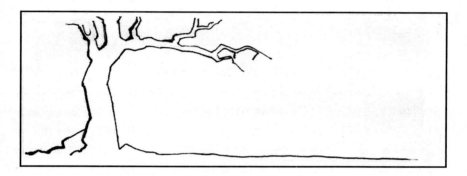

Always eager to please, Chuck was off his mount in a flash, snatching the ill-fated hat, dusting and reshaping to make it all better before Archie regained his senses. If those cracked ribs slowed Archie down, that severe bruising to the ego did nothing to help. Nonetheless, Archie arranged for alternative means back down the mountain. Poor horse Rocky has been *persona non-gratis* ever since. I heard nothing of what happened to the Big Spender.

Since that time, there have been largely unsubstantiated rumors of a certain photograph; of a certain horse, with a certain someone's *pistola* aimed straight at his head. Fortunately for horse Rocky, he has since been given a good home with folks that live far far away.

If ever a person hoped for good fortune in starting out as a camp cook, I could not have faired better with this group. Three daddies and their exceptional kids. Miss Belle, Tucker and young Will were well-behaved Southern children who always *"thanked me for the good food M'am."* They would not have dared omit the courtesy, and I would not have dared ask if they meant it.

During that short time I witnessed the humor of these men introducing their children to grown-up vices, under supervision of course. In the old traditions, it was hoped that a kid who learns about such things at home wasn't as likely to go wild with it later on. BRING ON THE CIGARS!

Miss Belle was thoroughly unimpressed and trotted off to more fitting pursuits. But young Will was mesmerized with envy as the older Tucker chomped away on that unlit cigar (pronounced C-gar). Finally Will boomed, **"Daddy, I want me a C-GAR."** (*You DO son….Why?*)

"'Cause I'm a MAN!"

Miss Belle made a fairly good tomboy, keeping the boys in line and spurring games of hide and seek well past sundown, though her true nature did surface when it came time for the morning horse wrangle. The boys liked to get up early and help Chuck gather the horses from pasture (the correct term would be "wrangle"). Anxious as they were, good manners dictate that they wait for ladies. Miss Belle required time to wash up and "put on the do." A virtual eternity in boy minutes, and there was some serious pouting going on. Years later, I imagine Miss Belle has blossomed into a lovely young woman, but I bet the days of Darby Mountain remain fondly in her heart.

Tucker is featured on Chuck's most recent brochure along with his all time favorite horse, Bud. Tucker is a natural rider who dreams of returning to work for Chuck when he gets older. He has been working on his sulky cowboy demeanor ever since. As Chuck notes, "the best thing for the inside of a boy is the outside of a horse. Makes perfect sense to me.

OLD SOUTH PEACH COBBLER

1 stick	butter
1 C.	sugar
1 C.	milk
1 C.	self-rising flour
2 C.	fresh Georgia peaches, peeled & sliced
	(I recently substituted canned peaches, and while this is no doubt sacrilege to the tradition, not one crumb of the Cobbler remained.)

Melt butter in 2-quart casserole. In a separate bowl, blend flour, sugar and milk; pour over melted butter. Do not stir. Pour peaches all over the top. Bake at 375°- 400° F degrees for approximately 40 minutes.

Serve hot with Caramel Sauce, Ice Cream or Whipped Cream

CARAMEL SAUCE

1 C.	brown or cane sugar, packed
½ C.	whipping cream
¼ C.	Karo syrup

Combine all ingredients in large saucepan. Cook briefly over medium heat, stirring constantly, then reduce heat to low and simmer for about 5 minutes.

HOW TO CATCH A POLAR BEAR

Chuck Thornton has a special way with the young ones who visit his world. Whether telling a joke or demonstrating a slick way to dismount bareback (will someone please remind the horse to keep its head down, huh?) Chuck pays extra attention to the kids. In turn, they generally idolize him and stay close to his side.

This is one of Chuck's favorite little wrangler jokes — all told in good fun though it has raised a few eyebrows now and then. Its about the lost art of catching polar bears......

> *"Hey kids, do ya want ta' know how to catch a*
> *polar bear?*
>
> *Well, ya cut a hole in the ice, and surround it with*
> *peas. Then go hide and wait...*
>
> *When the polar bear bends over to take a <u>pea</u>,*
> *ya kick it in the <u>ice hole</u>!"*

While the kids hear it one way, the fun part is hearing them retell it to their parents, who hear it quite another way.

> *"Hey Dad, do you wanna know how to catch a polar bear?"*

*It is not recommended that you try this at home.

FANCY POLAR PEAS*

Just the perfect bait for the unsuspecting polar bear. Visualize whirled peas!

2 T.	butter
1 slice	bacon
2 C.	peas; fresh shelled
8	tiny onions
¼ C.	cream
	salt & pepper to taste
	dash of dill if you like

Cook butter and bacon for 5 minutes. Remove bacon, add peas and some water; boil about 15 minutes. Also boil onions in a little salted water. Crumble bacon. Drain peas and onions. Combine peas, onion, bacon, cream and seasonings. Heat through and serve.

* Recipe from www.hugs.org

BODACIOUS ROASTED POTATOES

And why not some Bodacious Roasted Potatoes to go with those Fancy Polar Peas?

3 lg.	red or russet potatoes, washed and cut in 1" chunks
1 lg.	onion, cut in large chunks
	water
	pepper & salt
	thyme
	olive oil

Coat large casserole dish with Canola spray or oil. Spread potatoes and chunks of onion in dish. Add water just to cover the bottom of pan. Drizzle olive oil lightly over vegetables and sprinkle spices. Bake at 325°F for approx. 40 minutes, or until potatoes are tender and browned on the edges. These could easily be modified for Dutch oven cooking over coals as well.

For variations, try sweet potatoes with chopped red pepper, and add rosemary to the spicing.

MAKE **HIS** A MULE!

Ah yes, the mules. "Halfbreeds" as some outfitters call them. For those who aren't better acquainted with ole' long ears, a mule is a cross between a jack (donkey) and a horse — and they are always one of a kind 'cause you can't never breed a mule. (Mules are usually borne sterile, and thus, truly cannot be bred.)

Chuck has a particular love for his half-breed darlin's, preferring nothing better than a good riding mule. Says the mule is the "Cadillac of Horses" though a lot of folks would rather be hogtied and drug through sheep dip than be seen riding one. Ain't dignified. Maybe brings to mind images of Festus from the old Western Gunsmoke. Fine with Chuck, he has a handsome buckskin mule by the name of John Wayne that sports a heart-shaped marking right smack on his behind. Feel free to derive any special meaning you like from this.

Oh yes, Chuck'll be smooth riding up that rugged mountain terrain while y'all are getting' whiplash on your more fashionable mount. (Be sure and dress right for the occasion) Seriously now, mules are extra mindful of where they step whereas horses tend to clomp along, which kind of takes it out of your hide after a good long ride. You might not think this of worthy note until you stop and realize, you still have that long ride to the trailhead to contend with. In case of saddle sores, a few well-placed maxipads will do the trick…

So while the mule may be viewed as inherently comical on the outside, they command a certain amount of respect from those who know them better. Not only is the mule a smooth-footed mountain steed, they are intelligent — sometimes dangerously so. Young Josh found that out the hard way when he reckoned to ride old Tommy after making fun of his fat little mule belly all day long. Josh hit the dirt, repeatedly — and with little effort on Tommy's part. Josh just laughed – I swear that boy had no fear whatsoever.

One afternoon while taking advantage of a little solitude (sitting in yonder mountain meadow painting a small oil landscape) one of the mules came careening down the mountain trail with Chuck's prized, custom-made, hand-tooled saddle a'clang banging underneath. Knowing Chuck as an expert horseman, I could only imagine what catastrophe must have taken place to unseat him. I frankly never expected to see the day.

I jumped up and ran towards the cut-off, hoping to catch that mule before it could get back to camp, when yet another mule came crashing along behind it. TWO mules. Oh Lordy, it must be a bad wreck. There was only one saving grace here — my overweight form puffing down the trail left little time to fully contemplate the full magnitude of possibilities.

Well the mules made it all the way back to camp with me wheezing and straggling at the rear. I jumped on one of them and attempted to sally forth, which would have been more successful if the danged thing hadn't set her sights on staying in camp. I procured a riding twitch, uttered a few magic words that only mules can understand and we were OFF. By now I was nearly panicked with worry.

As luck would have it, the gang was not far from camp, and for the most part everyone was all right. Turned out Chuck had switched mounts with the fidgety Josh, who was complaining about something which I cannot recall. Josh then chose a particularly steep slope to do something stupid, which lead to his unseating in a most startling manner. At which point his Father, an uptight micromanaging sort of fellow, bailed his mount trying to rescue his beloved son. As relieved as I was to find everyone in tact, I did note that the Father was not exactly thankful. The term SOB did come to mind. Had I not nearly suffered a coronary on his son's behalf? Had not his foolish son caused Chuck's fine saddle a deep gouging? HELLO! This is somewhat akin to sacrilege in the West. Gets right up there with messing with the hat and other offenses. Perhaps I should have slipped something in his coffee? Be assured, the dear man departed camp with nary a case of the trots, regardless of what thoughts may have passed my mind. I wholeheartedly subscribe to the slightly rearranged old idiom that "*time wounds all heels*." Now back to the mules.

Interestingly, though mules are often smarter than their equine counter parts, they tend to closely bond with horses and do not generally want to go any- where without them. Mulesalso do not want to be left behind, which is why we often had to halter and tie all the mules prior to daily trail rides. Otherwise, they would jump the highest fence or crawl under it if need be, to get to their beloved horses. If Chuck tethered just one particular horse in an open field (usually the dominating mare) and left ten mules to roam free, likely they would be nearby in the morning.

I later learned of another formidable aspect of the mule, specifically the fa- mous Missouri mules, which are workhorse-sized mules bred and trained to work in powerful teams. A wrangler in the Bridger-Teton Wilderness remi- nisced of one fateful night when a grizzly wandered into their pastures. The two teams got together and drove that grizzly straight out of there! Now would YOU chase a grizzly?

An important side note: mules quite often detest dogs. No offense intended to you dog lovers, but one well-placed kick can be pretty hard on man's best friend. Please do keep your dog away from the mules or you might not have it very long. Chuck's favorite mule joke:

> Q: *"Why do baby mules take 10 months to gestate?*
> A: *Takes a month longer to hatch those ears!"*

I know — it is pitiful joke. But blame that one on Mr. Thornton. As much humor as I may find in mules, I do live by one credo — do all your teasing away from those sensitive ears or your time may come.

MULE BUTTER

1 pint	whipping cream
1 tsp.	salt
1	mule

One of the all time favorite camp treats was to make fresh homemade butter for the guests — especially considering that most everything we consume is purchased readymade off the shelf. In this age, most people have never made their own butter, much less seen it made. This simple deed never failed to fascinate my captive audience.

The key to making excellent mule butter is.... the longer the trail ride the better the butter — there is nothing like a good 30-mile pack trip to rattle and shake that whipping cream right into shape. Just pack the cartons into your pack panniers (uncooled) and let the mules do the work. By the time you get to your destination, a good 10 minutes of vigorous agitating on your part will likely be all that is necessary to finish the job. Simply transfer the whipping cream into an empty jar with a snug lid, add salt, and shake your booty. At some point, it will be so thick that it will be hard to shake at all — not to worry, you are almost done. Just shake it as hard as you can, or find some rugged individual who is a willing participant. When the butter separates, pour off the buttermilk and save for biscuits. Butter is now ready to serve.

For those of us who do not have a mule or a pack trip scheduled in the near future, this can be done at home as well. The key is that the whipping cream needs to sit out for a good part of the day at room temperature. Same procedure applies, and it is just as fun.

PORNOGRAPHIC ROW

The history of the American West is filled with stories of peoples from distant lands who came to fulfill their dreams. They sought land, wealth and a way of life. Most indigenous cultures were swept aside by greed while other cultures were boonswaggled into becoming labor for the benefit of the cause. In most cases, it was a life without women.

One culture, known for its expert "sheepmanship," is the Basque sheepherders. For centuries, these men have been known to tend flocks far and wide through vast high countries of the West. I have heard stories about the lives of those men — often tending thousands of sheep that at any given time might choose to divide and wander. Night and day, the bear and coyote pose constant threat, plaguing the tired guardians of the flock and their sheep dogs for a little fluffy snack. Tufts of fur were all that remained in their wake.

Living in the high elevations left the sheepherders vulnerable to Wyoming's infamous sudden winds and summer storms. In those parts, snow can fall heavy and trap herder's on the mountain, even in July! Yes, the life of a sheepherder is not for the meek. By today's standards, both the pay and the rewards are relatively small, with virtually no hope of a tip in sight. The days are long, the nights longer, the work is exhaustive and above all, there are NO women! Hence life in the hills was a lonely prospect, and besides, there are no flattering songs written about sheepherders.

There are still a few Basque herders around Lake Alice, high above Chuck's summer camp. Nice fellows who speak little English and subsist on mutton. Always looking for a better opportunity, one of them keeps working on Chuck to hire him. Indeed, every time Chuck rides by with his guests, the fellow will herd him into the makeshift tent and ply him with wine. Fool should have known better than to develop a crush on Chuck's fetching blond daughter Misty —

On one of those high mountain slopes lies further testament to the sheepherder's blues ... a grove of aspen, replete with carvings dating back over thirty years.

We call it Pornographic Row.

SPICY LAMB CHILI*

¾ lb.	lean ground lamb
1 med.	red onion, chopped
2 cloves	garlic, crushed
2 lg.	red peppers, chopped
2 tsp.	chili powder
2 tsp.	cumin
¼ tsp.	salt
½ tsp.	cayenne pepper
½ tsp.	black pepper
3-8 oz. cans	tomato sauce
2-5 oz. cans	dark red kidney beans
1-15 oz. can	tomatoes, diced & undrained
1-15 oz.can	chicken broth
2-4 oz. cans	green chilies, drained
	olive oil

Heat large Dutch oven with olive oil over medium-high heat until hot. Add lamb, garlic and onion; cook until brown, stirring to crumble lamb. Drain and remove lamb mixture from pan. Clean drippings from pan with paper towel. Return lamb, garlic and onions to pan. Stir in chili powder, cumin, salt, cayenne pepper, black pepper, tomato sauce, kidney beans, chopped to-matoes, chicken broth and green chilies. Bring to a boil. Reduce heat, and simmer 15-20 minutes, stirring occasionally. Serve hot.

* Sourced from www.wpr.org/zorba/recipes

SUNKEN SHIP SPRINGS

The Poker Creek trail into Lake Alice is an excursion into parts of Wyoming that most people will never see. Mainly, because they can't get there by car. Among the many wonders is a natural spring, maybe 25 feet diameter and 65 plus feet deep, overflowing with clear icy water. Down inside is a huge fallen tree that looks like the mast of a sunken ship. The locals have a variety of names for the thing, including Sunken Ship Springs. Personally, I call it the Hell Hole — you might think the devil lived down there by the way some folks react to the thought of swimming in it.

No respectable cowboy would dip his big toe in that spring for fear it might be his last act on God's green earth. Well at least Chuck wouldn't – no SIR! A man ud' hate to THINK of the terrors that lie waiting for him ... in the Hell Hole.

One day I set out to clear a section of trail of its plentiful rocks, as Chuck and the guests headed out for a trail ride. We arranged to meet at the spring for lunch. By the time I arrived, the trail dust and midday sun had taken toll, and a dip in that spring looked pretty good to me. Chuck was not impressed. In fact, he looked quite uncomfortable, kind of like a guy who has been sitting in wet shorts a bit too long. The guests laughed, albeit nervously. Even I hesitated, thinking maybe it was better left alone? I supposed the spectacle of my drowning would not exactly be good entertainment for the guests. But I was parched in a way that no amount of water could quench. I am a genuine Northern girl, from Maine nonetheless where the water is not reputed to be warm. I had been swimming in it all my life and LOVING it. Besides which, I am not accustomed, as a woman, to being told I cannot do something that seems perfectly reasonable to me.

CHUCK: *"Well I guess you know Cookie, I am not too happy with you swimmin' in that spring."*

ME: *"And I guess you know Chuck, you ain't near old enough to be ma' Daddy, and even if you was, you'd know I NEVER listen to* **NUTHIN'** *ma' Daddy says!"*

CHUCK: *"Well what if you get caught up on that tree down there?"*

ME   *"I was plannin' on swimming, not <u>sinking</u> Chuck!"*

CHUCK: *"Well I am not comin' in after ya!"*

And so the dialogue continued until I dove in, leaving Chuck to his demons. The bottom line being he didn't dare jump in that water because he did not have the benefit of a goodly amount of insulation to protect him from the cold… whereas I had plenty. (OK — so I admitted it.)

Even so, let me be the first to tell you, that sucker was COLD! And upon diving into it, one can only hope to surface before that involuntary GaaaaSP of cold fully registers. But as you may guess, I was not sucked down into the Hell Hole by the dreaded Swamp Thang, nor did Chuck subsequently suffer a coronary on my account. The guests fortunately were amused, and even took pictures. I do not lie.

So add that to yer stories boys! The way they talked you might think I was only one to ever swim in that spring. But I rather doubt it – there are lots of hardheaded women in the West!

SAUCY COWBOY DIP

Now doesn't this sound appropriate? Eat enough of this bean dip, and you may have your very own cowboy bubble bath!

2 lg. cans	black beans, rinsed and drained
½ C	prepared, low-sodium chicken broth
3 tsp.	fresh lemon or lime juice
¼ C.	onion, finely chopped
1	Roma tomato
4 cloves	garlic, finely minced
1 med.	jalapeno pepper, seeded and finely chopped
3 T.	fresh cilantro, chopped
½ tsp.	salt

Mash beans in bowl. Add chicken broth, lemon or lime juice, onions, tomato, garlic, Jalapeno, cilantro and salt. Chill for one hour to blend flavors and serve with warm tortillas or tortilla chips.

SKINNY DIP

On a hot summer day, one good dip deserves another. Here's a skinny alternative, sans bubbles.

10 oz.	frozen spinach
1-8 oz. pkg.	farmer cheese
½ C.	light mayonnaise
¼ C.	green onions/scallions, minced
¼ C.	parsley, chopped
2 T.	lemon juice
½ tsp.	salt
	pepper to taste

Defrost spinach and squeeze out excess water. Using blender or food processor, blend spinach and farmer cheese. Add remaining ingredients and blend well. Chill until ready to serve.

COOKIE TURNS INTO A PUMPKIN

One day we encountered some of Chuck's old time acquaintances at the trailhead. They were a motley bunch, eyes all asquint from years of Wyoming sun; men of varying vintage dressed in their best old dungs and riding gear in preparation for the yearly Fish Campout at Lake Alice. We were poised to return to Lake Alice ourselves, with the next batch of guests nearly rabid in anticipation of the trip. In parting, I was introduced as "this year's Cookie," which won a rapid oath that they would be sure to drop in and check out my cooking soon as they could get there. Just as quickly I quipped that I *cooked nothing but "Weens & Beanies," and they wasn't all that good neither."* On that note, we headed off.

As promised, it was not long before the bunch showed up for a visit. In fact, I recollect it was that very same evening. How do I know after all these years? Why because my eyes are just now becoming unglued from their sockets?

To explain, on the days we packed the guests into camp we will rise at 5:00 a.m., packing, sorting and preparing for the trip. We will drive 40 miles into the trailhead, saddle and pack the mules and horses, and ride for another three to four hours before we ever hit camp where we will unpack, settle the guests and cook dinner. By the time that day is done, it is 11:00 p.m. in the evening, and all hands are ready to drop. All this on the heels of a the previous day's pack out, only in reverse. So imagine how it might be if a group of good old boys were to show up for a visit and just hang on beyond all good sense? Imagine further that you personally sleep in the cook tent, which happens to be the social hub of the establishment, and that you do not GET to sleep until every last one of them vamooses? Yessuh, that is just how it happened. And I can remember exactly how it felt trying to keep my eyes open that evening. Got so I would walk out into the night just to slap myself awake, hoping that when I returned they'd be collecting for departure. Nothing doing. It had been some time since the fellows had visited with Chuck, and it seems there was just endless stuff to talk about, the importance of which I could not figure.

My eyes glazed over as I mused on an old French trapper's joke about a toilet seat that got painted and just would not dry for weeks on end. The joke went on for some time about the sufferings experienced, waiting for that seat to dry. I felt somewhat connected to that feeling just now, waiting for these fellas to evaporate. Fantasized about the variety of Halloween masks I would like to sport, just to see if anyone noticed? Seemed like the Hoover Dam could dry in the time it took for these boys to get a clue, even Chuck was winding down and you could see how he would tactfully let silence hang at the end of a sentence... but if I have learned anything about folks in the back country, once they get around to visit they like to make it worthwhile.

At this point, our polite guests were also struggling to stay awake — the froth being somewhat cooled on their anticipation. My eyes were now pretty much crossed — but the fellows freshened their drinks and settled in for a good extended visit. Lord, this was a tough call as there are certain matters of protocol in camp hospitality, and it would not do to embarrass Chuck. Still, it looked like hell was near about to freeze over before these fellows would think to hit the trail. I stepped outside and debated with the devil on my shoulder, then stepped back into the tent, took a good yawn and a stretch, and announced without apology, *"Y'all might want to be heading out....It is nigh to midnight, and pretty soon, Cookie turns into a pumpkin and I guarantee you, it is NOT a pretty sight!"*

While I cannot attest to what visions might have run through their minds at that moment, I can vouch for the fact that my kitchen and all its inhabitants was cleared in mere seconds flat. The look of gratitude from some parties did not go unnoticed.

HONEY PUMPKIN PIE

If you're going to turn into a pumpkin, you might as well make it sweet!

1-16 oz. can	pumpkin
¾ C.	honey
1 tsp.	ground cinnamon
½ tsp.	salt
½ tsp.	ginger
¼ tsp.	nutmeg
¼ tsp.	cloves
3	eggs
1 can	evaporated milk (2/3 C.)
½ C.	milk

Combine pumpkin, honey, cinnamon, salt, ginger, nutmeg and cloves. Add eggs and beat into pumpkin mixture with a fork. Stir in evaporated milk and regular milk. Prepare pastry and fit into a 9-inch pie plate; flute edges to hold the filling. Do not prick the shell. Place pie shell on oven rack, pour in filling. Bake at 375°F for 55 to 60 minutes or until pie is set.
Cool before serving.

PUMPKIN BREAD*

A popular old tyme favorite…

1 2/3 C.	flour
1 tsp.	baking soda
¼ tsp.	baking powder
¾ tsp.	salt
½ tsp.	ground cloves
½ tsp.	ground cinnamon
½ tsp.	ground nutmeg
½ tsp.	ground allspice
¾ C.	sugar
½ C.	oil
2	eggs
1 C.	canned pumpkin
1 C.	raisins (optional)

Sift flour, soda, powder, salt and spices. In another bowl beat the sugar and oil until smooth. Beat in eggs one at a time. Stir in pumpkin and flour mixture. Add raisins. Turn into loaf pan and bake at 350°F for 60 minutes. Makes one loaf.

* Sourced from Arielle's Recipe Archives at http://recipes.alastra.com ~ an excellent and well-organized collection of recipes.

PAYBACK

Did'ya ever hear of that old saying about "payback?" Well into everyone's life, a little payback must fall. And in the hills, the possibilities are nearly endless.

It was the end of August when the summer trips have ended and winter will soon reclaim the mountains and the hidden places. At this point, Darby Mountain condenses its operations into the lower camp where hunting season will soon kick into gear. And so it happened that Chuck, John Fellow and I rode into Lake Alice to pack up the summer camp.

First, let me say that Chuck and John Fellow are pretty good-natured fellows, so it was an enjoyable time. But anyone who has ever endured a trip with THAT pair can vouch for how much razzing I suffered. Which was not all that bothersome — it only relieved me of any guilt I might otherwise have felt when serving it right BACK! After a good couple days I announced they could tease me ALL they wanted… it wouldn't bother me a BIT when payback came around! I am saying this as John Fellow and I are holding the corners to the large canvas tent while Chuck prepared to take down the frame from the inside.

CHUCK: *"OH, Does that mean yer a'plottin' against us*
            Cookie?"

ME   *"Nope. Don't need to. Payback just has a*
        WaaAY of happenin."

Just then John Fellow let go of his corner, and taking the cue from my elders, I let go too. Chuck, unfortunately, had just walked into the heavy tent, which promptly collapsed on his head. OOPsy. Hadn't realized our ropes were the only thing holding the tent up or I might have thought twice afore dropping it on Chuck. Sure was a sight – our fearless leader valiantly fighting off the tent monster. Kind of like a couple of cats in a potato sack. Miraculously, he emerged, a bit red-faced and flustered, but with the hat intact. Chuck never

likes the hat to come off.

No point in playing innocent now — I could not have hid the smirk on my face for all the Copenhagen in Wyoming; any more than stifle the chortles that soon followed. It was about the funniest thing I had ever seen. Chuck snapped accusingly, *"JUST look at ya with that big grin on yer face!"* By the way he was huffing and puffing with that *madder than a wet hen* look to his eyes, I probably should have been afraid. But with hunting season just starting my life expectancy was somewhat assured – for a little while. And besides, you just never knew – maybe I did have it in for him? That little bit of doubt was my ace in the hole. Wouldn't hurt to have Chuck watching his back for a while, and I could sure have some fun with that! Any cook worth her salt can exact a fair bit of influence on the camp. A couple of extra special surprise goodies in the lunch bag … dog kibble does nicely … maybe the cellophane mistakenly gets left on the cheese… toilet paper mysteriously disappears at just the point when everyone but the cook has come down with the trots…

Oh yes, with just a little creativity, payback just happens.

BUTTERFINGERS (wOOPS!)*

½ C.	margarine
½ C.	sugar
½ C.	brown sugar
1	egg
½ C.	peanut butter
½ tsp.	vanilla

1 C.	flour
½ tsp.	soda
¼ tsp.	salt
1 C.	quick oats

Combine margarine, sugar, brown sugar, egg, peanut butter and vanilla. In separate bowl, combine dry ingredients, add to mixture. Spread mixture in 9 x 13 pan and bake at 350°F for 20 minutes.

1 pkg.	milk chocolate chips

Remove from oven, spread chocolate chips on top and place back in oven for several minutes until melted. Remove from oven and spread chocolate with knife.

TOPPING

½ C.	confectioner's sugar
¼ C.	peanut butter
2-4 T.	milk

Drizzle topping over top and serve in squares.

*Recipe from me Mum.

WIMP AND BUD

Wimp   Bud

"Wimp" (short for Wenzel) was the first moose hunter of the season. Bud, his lifelong friend, came along for the ride. And so two seasoned old characters showed up from Wisconsin one day, big goofy grins and a freezer trailer in tow. Both of them, you must know, were in their 70's — a far sight older than the cheese they brought as gifts. The first words out of Wimp's mouth were *"If I can't tease the cook I'm LEAVING!"* Oh Lordy. That infectious smile of his said I was IN for it!

Our original plan had been to pack Wimp into a "spike camp" (a temporary hunt camp consisting of a small canvas tent, wood stove and simple provisions) by horse. As it turned out, we were blessed with an early winter that year, with a fresh foot of new snow lying heavy and wet on the mountains. The boys were more than happy to stay at Chuck's ranch and hunt from the truck. (I expect that cold wet trailride up the mountain would have been a bit tough on their senior behinds.)

First day out, that old character got his moose — with a cross bow no less. I'll never know how they got it all in the back of the truck, but they drove up with the legs sticking out like the moose was doing the backstroke or something. Up until then, I had never seen Bullwinkle up close — they are an awesome big thing.

I later learned that Wimp's moose was nearly blind due to a parasite that commonly afflicts the moose species. That summer I had seen a female with two calves – blind and confused in some rancher's pasture. Slowly the three of them were starving.

Wimp was a humble man and I do not imagine it would have wounded his pride to know that the moose had been disadvantaged. Truth was, that poor moose would have suffered through the winter until it eventually starved. Wimp had both saved it from a worse fate and provided food for his son and grandchildren, with whom he lived.

When it came time for the "terrible two" to go, we were fairly sure we could not stand for them to leave. They had become like family, entertaining us with their stories and silly jokes and there is nothing so heartening as two old buds off on an adventure. They had already won over the locals at the town's only drinking establishment, and Bud had tried his best to dupe me with his old Indian Love Stone joke, which I expect would have landed me a fairly embarrassing wet smooch if I had been a tad more gullible. One of those two clowns even slipped a goofy fishing hat into my car as a goodbye gift. I kept it for several years before passing it on to just the right person.

Wimp and Bud are fondly remembered as two good souls who leave a place a fair bit richer than what they found it. Chuck had an especially tender spot for both of them and wondered if he would be that spry at 75?

Meanwhile, he coveted the cheese, which was never seen again.

HUNTER'S STEW

Guaranteed to warm old bones on the coldest of winter days, this stew can be modified depending upon the contents of your refrigerator.

	olive oil or canola oil
3	cloves garlic, minced
2 lb.	stew beef, cubed
1 T.	crushed basil
	black pepper
6	green onions/scallions, chopped with tops
1 lg.	onion, chopped
½	green pepper, chopped
½	red pepper, chopped
1 sm.	jalapeno, chopped (optional)
1-16 oz. can	crushed tomato
4 lg.	potatoes, washed and cubed
2 lg.	carrots, peeled and sliced ¼"
1-16 oz.	beer, any brand
1 T.	thyme
1 tsp.	fennel seed
	black pepper, garlic & onion powder & Tabasco to taste.

Heat oil on high in Dutch oven. Sear beef, then add garlic and spices. Reduce heat and add onions and peppers. Sauté until onions are clear.

Add beer, and water to cover along with crushed tomato, vegetables and remaining spices. Bring to boil and reduce heat to simmer for 40 minutes, or until vegetables are cooked. Adjust salt and spices to taste.

CHEESE SOUP

And another warming soup for those who LUV cheese!

3 T.	unsalted butter
1 med.	onion, finely chopped
3 T.	flour
7 C.	milk, broth, or water
1½ lb.	firm Cheddar cheese, coarsely grated
¼ tsp.	garlic powder
	Bouquet Garni* (small bundle of herbes tied together with string and enclosed in piece of cheese cloth. Suggest ½ tsp. of thyme for this soup.)
6-1" slices	French bread, toasted and cubed.

Melt butter in a 4-quart pot over medium heat. Add onion and stir the mixture for 5 minutes. Add flour and stir 5 minutes longer, being careful not to let the butter burn.

Whisk in liquids, bring to a boil. Add Bouquet Garni, lower heat and simmer gently for 10 minutes. Remove Bouquet Garni, turn off heat and whisk in the cheese.

Ladle soup into serving crocks, reserving 1 cup. Arrange bread cubes over each crock, ladle the remaining soup over the bread and sprinkle with the remaining cheese.

If serving the soup right away, bake the crocks in a 400°F oven until they start to bubble and brown on top — about 10 minutes. If you have made the soup in advance, bake at 325°F for about 25 minutes.

WISCONSIN CHEDDAR BACON PUFFS*

1/3 C.	butter
1 C.	water
1 C.	flour
4	eggs
½ C.	sharp Cheddar, grated
4 slices	bacon, cooked and crumbled
2 T.	grated Parmesan

Boil butter and water. Add flour all at once, stirring vigorously. Continue stirring until mixture forms a ball that does not separate. Remove from heat and let cool about 10 minutes.

Preheat oven to 400°F degrees.

Beat in eggs, one at a time. Beat in cheese and bacon. Drop dough by well-rounded tablespoons into a 6" ring on greased cookie sheets, leaving about ¼ " between balls of dough. Sprinkle with Parmesan.

Bake approximately 30 minutes until golden brown. Serve warm.

*Sourced from www.hugs.org, another fabulous collection of recipes.

THE COUCH KILLER

"Say, do ya mind if I clean my gun in the cook tent?"

I should have nipped it in the bud right then, but I didn't. And so a straggling hunter came in from the cold to clean his gun in my cook tent one morning. He was a nice enough fellow, a college professor from California with a Master in Theatre. And MY how he LUVed to TALK! To say that Russ was a little green about the woods would be an understatement. But then who was I to talk? Had I not been perched behind a computer with a telephone near surgically attached to my ear not a year before? Naturally I was not thrilled to have him playing with his gun in such close proximity, but at least I could keep a watch on him. The walls of a canvas tent do not offer much in the way of bullet protection, and a gun is just as dangerous in the next tent over.

So Russ commenced to tinker with his rifle while I grumpily set about making a late breakfast for him. I had just leaned over to light the propane burner when kaBANNNG-O – there was a helluva noise. (Dang, I never did trust those propane stoves!) My head was filled with a loud roaring commotion, which returns at odd moments without warning to this day. After the roar subsided, I stood up to survey the damage. There was Russ, standing over the couch with a smoking rifle – one of those high-powered Remington numbers, which I had developed a new appreciation for of late. We were speechless.

"JEeeZUS Russ, YOU SHOT THE COUCH … and tha' PORK CHOPS! Dammit whadidyado that for? Sure enough, the end of the couch hung tattered (made a dandy beer holder) and the bullet had ripped clean through Chuck's' antique turkey roaster (an heirloom from Mother Thornton) where the chops were thawing (I'm quite certain they was already DEAD.) The bullet had continued on out of the tent and through a cooler outside, shredding the cheese as it passed through (Golly, is that how the cowboys make Swiss?).

Russ jumped back, pointing at the offending gun and shrieked, *"IT WASN'T SUPPOSED TO __DO__ THAT!"* Really, you would think that gun had flat out betrayed him, when all it did was highlight how he still had a thing or two to learn about it. All those years of studying gun literature and practicing did not amount to a pile of chew just then. A second hunter in the neighboring tent was bellowing like a bull, *"IS EVERYONE OK IN THERE?"* and demanding a full accounting of the situation. (I suspect he had been taking a nap and quite possibly had wet his pants.) Our poor dude was in full panic mode and if he could have vaporized himself just then I believe he would have clicked his expensive Cabella boots and been gone.

"I want to go home NOW! Take me to the trailhead NOW!!!" (Stomping of foot for emphasis, which made his belly jiggle in a most comical way.) But it was too late to salvage even one modicum of male machismo.

You see, Russ's greatest joy of the hunt was not the kill, the Western food, or even sidling up to Trigger and getting saddle sores to prove he was a man. No, Russ's Number One biggest thrill was the STORIES. Those tall tales for which sportsmen are well noted – that nightly rationing of bullshit to top off the day, soothe the weariness and send them to bed chuckling. Each evening, Russ showed up for dinner, eagerly clutching his journal and praying for a new story to record. Now he had BECOME the story and it was too much to bear. More than anything, I believe he wanted to be accepted and to fit in. Now he was fairly certain that ole' Chuck was going to pistol whup him and banish his quivering hide from camp – forever. Naturally, he wanted to die.

Meanwhile, our one road out of camp was nearly impassable after a week of snow and rain. Shit pie. Poop Soup. Twelve inches of smarmy muck. Well and beyond my meager 4-wheel driving capabilities. Regardless of Russ's insistence that I drive him out, swamping Chuck's truck in the *mud hole of no return* would not exactly sweeten his mood for the news of this morning's event. Might just as well pack my own bags while I was at it.

"Now Russ, cool off and think on it for a spell. If you hightail it now, you will never be able to return and YOU KNOW IT!" Even in the face of total humiliation, Russ could not bear the prospect of missing next year's stories. Oh how it tor-

tured him, as those *fight or flight* urges kicked in. I left him with that thought while I snuck off for a good laugh, which was my due.

Later, the other hunter, whose name shall mercifully remain unknown, (besides which, I cannot remember it) was trying to be helpful by *"tracking the bullet"* (shhhhhhh) which involved a lot of puffing and strutting importantly about — a fair tribute to the common barnyard rooster. Recognizing this to be one of those male rituals best not disturbed, I stifled myself. Even when he pinpointed a couple of large rivet holes in a nearby tent as the exit tracks of the bullet. NOT a word! This was a man of such stature that he had literally pulled his horse off'n its feet just trying to mount for the hunt. Kind of like trying to perch a cannonball on top a sawhorse. Got so by the end of the hunt, his horse's eyes buggered out at the mere sight of him. I figured my life expectancy remained reasonably decent so long as I kept quiet—so long as I could help it.

It is fair to note that I did try to contain myself. Honest I did. But alas, the absurdity of the situation was not lost, even on Russ. Just then he glanced my way and, recognizing the giggles about to erupt, actually dared to <u>wag his finger</u> threateningly. But it was too late.

I must admit, Russ took it well when I suggested that we strap a pair of elk antlers onto the couch and maybe take some trophy shots (smile pretty). Worse yet, each batch of hunters to return to camp let him have it all anew (smile real pretty). Our valiant hunter remained stoic and good-natured — probably because he imagined we would stop sooner or later. However, this was a bit of a delicate situation, Russ being a paying guest and all. If it had been a normal group of guys out in the woods, they would have felt welcomed to chew him out, maybe deck him a few times. Every hunter knows that a misfired gun can reap deadly results. As it was, they had to find other means of getting the message across, and relentless humor was the next best option. Rest assured, Russ got the message and I wager he never dry fired his rifle during the cleaning process again. I even bet he smartens up and counts his loads upon removing them the night before.

Later that day, Russ was lavishing compliments upon my exceptional roast turkey sandwiches (trying to change the subject), saying he had *enjoyed it so much, was there enough left over for another sandwich?* Not to impose, just point him to the turkey and he would make his own (after all, I nearly killed you). I paused to think and then realized the fate of the left over turkey. . .

Yes indeed – the bullet had claimed the leftover turkey on its ill-fated trip through the cooler as well.

"DAMMIT RUSS, YA SHOT THAT TOO!"

RUSS'S FAVORITE SHOTGUN TURKEY

1   roasting turkey, washed and trimmed of fat

      thyme
      basil
      onion powder
      black pepper
      or any of your favorite spices

      water
      dash of curry (optional for the broth)

Place turkey in roaster, cover top of legs and breasts with tinfoil to keep moist, add 2 inches of water to roasting pan. Lightly coat with spices. (A <u>small</u> amount of curry will fill out the flavor of the broth.)

Cover with lid and cook at 325°F for appropriate time according to weight. Baste occasionally, removing lid for remaining 15 minutes to brown. Save broth for gravy or soup stock.

PS. The secret is in the water, which steams the bird as it bakes, keeping it moist and infusing it with spices. Makes great leftover turkey sandwiches — so long as nobody shoots it up!

SWEET APPLE STUFFING

Add a chopped apple along with onion, and celery (optional) to your favorite stuffing mix.

GRAVY

After turkey is well done, skim off fat. Strain and pour off broth into saucepan. Add additional pepper, onion powder and soy sauce (or salt) to taste. Thicken with flour and water mixture as desired, using a whip to eliminate embarrassing lumps.

Giblets optional. I prefer to leave them out of gravy due to slightly bitter taste.

SHOTGUN TURKEY SOUP

This is my version of good old-fashioned Turkey Soup. If you are going to the trouble of cooking a full turkey dinner, and if you are inclined to take the extra time to cut all the turkey off the bone before serving, then you will have the makings of an excellent broth for soup.

Generally I set aside the bones in a stockpot, add leftover broth from having cooked the turkey with a few inches of water (see SHOTGUN TURKEY recipe), along with any leftover gravy. Add enough water (or commercial low fat chicken stock) to fully cover bones (fill pot ¾ full?) and boil the living hell out of it for an hour or so. Rehydrate as needed. If you have celery and onion available, throw in a couple of good-sized chunks of each and boil them too. Eventually, all this will be strained out of the broth and discarded.

Meanwhile, any of the following spices will sweeten the pot, or your basic poultry blend will work just as well:

1-2 tsp.	thyme
1-2 tsp.	basil
½ tsp.	curry

Set aside leftover turkey, as this will be added in the last 20 minutes of cooking. If cooked too long in the soup, turkey meat tends to disintegrate. Freeze turkey meat and broth if you are not planning to make the soup immediately.

In the best of circumstances, once the broth is made I prefer to let the fat settle on top, cool uncovered for an hour and freeze it. When I am ready to make soup, the fat can easily be removed. Otherwise, skim it off with a spoon or one of those turkey-basting thingamajigs. Not only do we not need the calories from fat, we don't need what is IN the fat (hormones, antibiotics and other lovely additives used by the poultry industry).

For vegetables, I often use the following:

6-7	scallions (also known as green onions)
1 lg.	onion, chopped
2 stocks	celery, including leaf, chopped
6 lg.	mushrooms, washed and sliced thick
1 med.	carrot, chopped (optional)
3 med.	potatoes
	egg noodles (store bought or Sandra's Egg Noodles)

Add vegetables to broth. Bring to boil, lower heat and simmer until potatoes are just beginning to soften.

Add a handful or two of egg noodles (depending on amount of broth) along with turkey meat and simmer another 10 minutes or until potatoes are fully cooked. Or use a half-cup of instant rice if preferred. Draw a half-cup of broth, let cool for tasting and adjust herbs and salt. Add thyme, basil, etc., as needed. If spicing or salt becomes too strong, dilute accordingly with water.

Optional Variations:

Left over mashed potatoes will thicken the soup.
Corn (either canned or fresh) is also a welcomed addition but use sparingly as too much can take over flavor of the soup. For a zestier variation, add a half-cup of salsa, green or red.

Serve hot with your favorite bread. Allow leftover to cool uncovered for an hour before placing in refrigerator. The soup will taste even better the next day!

SANDRA'S EGG NOODLES

Quick and easy!

3 C.	flour
5	eggs
½ C.	water, beer or milk

Roll thin on floured surface. Cut using pizza cutter and let dry. Add to broth as desired.

SHOTGUN TURKEY SALAD SANDWICHES

And of course, Russ's all time favorite Shotgun Turkey Salad Sandwiches. Buckshot optional.

	roasted turkey, cut in chunks
	mayonnaise
	finely chopped onion (optional)
dash	dried basil and/or thyme (optional)
dash	salt & paper to taste

Seems simple enough, but that special touch of roasting the turkey with water and spices makes this especially tasty.

SHOTGUN TURKEY POT PIE

Another leftover turkey option is the classic potpie, sans crust. I never did master crusts.

3 C.	turkey gravy
1 T.	cornstarch
½ C.	white wine (or cooking wine)
½ tsp.	black pepper
1 med.	onion
2 tsp.	dried thyme
3 C.	turkey, cut into large chunks
1-15 oz.	can of peas
1-15 oz.	can of sliced carrots, drained
	or 1 cup fresh carrots, sliced and pre-cooked
2 C.	potatoes, cut in chunks and pre-cooked
1- 8 oz. pkg.	Crescent Rolls (ready to bake)

Preheat oven to 375°F. Using wire whip, stir together gravy, cornstarch, cooking wine and black pepper until smooth and set aside.

Heat oil over medium-high heat. Add onion and thyme; cook until softened. Add reserved gravy mixture and bring to boil. Add turkey and vegetables; stir to coat evenly. Transfer to a 2-quart shallow baking dish.

Carefully remove crescent rolls from package, keeping dough in one sheet and pinching together seams to seal. Cut into 1-inch wide strips. Arrange pastry strips in a lattice pattern over filling. Bake for 20 to 25 minutes as directed, or until pastry is crisp and golden brown. Let cool slightly before serving.

Makes 6 servings.

THE WATERMELON CRAWL

One evening, the hunters returned from the hunt, excited with stories of success. It had been a tough week and they had suffered through many snowy days on horseback, leaving well before sunrise and arriving long after sundown. At 8,000 feet in elevation, September is basically winter in Wyoming – often a cold prospect. Needless to say, they were jolly well excited and this was cause for celebration. Soon the beer foamed and the Wild Turkey flew as one by one my band of merry hunters turned into bleary-eyed fools.

John Fellow seemed supremely happy that his fork both speared the potato chunk and subsequently found his mouth. Smutney was busy annoying his buddy Jay, and Chuck was in full red-faced talk mode. I sat back and watched. This was the best entertainment I'd had in a long time and I could hardly fault them, even if I DID have to wait till everyone left before I could hit the hay. Yes they were pretty mild compared to some hunt camps – and eventually the last of them headed off to bed and all was quiet – or so we thought.

The next morning everybody slept in. I headed out to break ice on the water barrel for the horses, when I spied something bobbing in the spring. Sure was a pretty sight with the morning sun twinkling on the water – what it could be? I found a stick and did a little fishing.

Well by golly it's Chuck's hat! And not just any hat – his genuine red wool Elmer Fudd hunting cap! I could not imagine what caused his parting ways with it. Chuck's kind of sensitive about the hat, and I thought sure he'd be torqued when he learned of its demise. Sacrilege! There must be a prankster loose in camp! With the late great prize dangling from the stick, I headed for Chuck's tent.

ME: *"KNOCK KNOCK. It's 7:00 am Chuck... do you KNOW where your HAT is?"*

CHUCK: *"**GaaAW** Cookie, I ain't even outta bed and you're **ONTA'** me!"*

This was not the response I expected. Surprise? Maybe a little outrage? But a hint of guilt — very puzzling. Figuring I would hear the story soon enough, I chuckled and deposited the soggy heap at his doorway.

Apparently, Chuck had not gone to bed, rather he had detoured down to a neighboring hunt camp for a nice howdy do. (They was playing the radio kind of loud, and it was a perfect excuse to harass them.) Now this is a camp where alcohol was known to run liberally. The young Turks saw Chuck coming and mixed him a few stiff ones, and this was Chuck's demise. You NEVER want to get Chuck talking unless you have a passal of spare time on your hands. Soon the alcohol did its magic on Chuck's tired body, and when it finally hit himthat it was time to leave, he could not walk. Years later, Chuck would admit that he actually passed out and hit the dirt. Now the boys, being such nice neighbors, decided to give Chuck a lift, piggyback style. Unfortunately, they too were in tough condition, and the road was icy and dark. Chuck ended up with a painful nosedive, bouncing down the road on his face with a few cracked ribs for his trouble. The boys found this rather funny.

At this point, the details become unclear. We will never know how Chuck got himself home... (did he do the "Watermelon Crawl?") And it is probably best not to discuss it in his presence, as he gets a decidedly taciturn look about him. But his partner and rooming buddy John Fellow can attest to a few incriminating details — like being rudely awaken to the sound of Chuck, attempting in vain to remove his leg gators. In the middle of the night, I imagine it was a bit like fingernails down the chalkboard — they've yet to make soundless Velcro. And then there was this guy "Ralphhhh" that Chuck was heard to be hollerin' for at odd times in the night. Never heard of no Ralph, and Chuck denies it. But John Fellow is not recanting a bit. I guess Ralph took off and left Chuck huddled up in the cold, because John Fellow finally had to go and retrieve him. As for the hat episode, we can only guess that Chuck must have gone for a little refresher in the spring and ended up with a nice Nordic dip instead. Whatever did happen, I slept right through it. But I know for certain that there is a little patch of road that bears the imprint of Chuck's face as testament to good times gone a'fowl. The hat was never seen again.

Now I was not exactly intending to be mean when I offered Chuck a little of the Hair o' the Dawg that morning. And it was not my fault that the hunters had specially requested a nice batch of oatmeal, which I had gone to the trouble of spicing with fruit and cinnamon. How was I to know that Mother Thornton had force-fed her brood oatmeal nearly every day of their natural-borne lives and that as an adult, Chuck was wont to hurl at the mere thought of it? I have heard about people like him. Even so, I could not help but push it Chuck's way a couple of extra times just for fun as I have never claimed to be an angel. Rest assured, it was a dry white season from then on, and Chuck was good behavior exemplified. Especially since it was some time before he could lift a saddle onto a horse without grimacing. Yes, a good long time to think about the virtues of sobriety, with a few well-placed reminders from yours truly.

Endnote: Before you gain an unflattering image of Chuck — allow me clarify that he is definitely NOT a drinking kind of guy, and it would be unfair to leave you with that impression. This was just one of those isolated incidents that caught up with him, and it struck me as just too comical to overlook. (Forgive me Chuck.)

CHUCK'S FAVORITE OATMEAL

(Better than Mother Thornton's)

5 C.	water
1	apple, cut in chunks (or canned pear)
¼ C.	raisins (optional)
¼ C.	chopped or slivered almonds
¼ tsp.	nutmeg & cinnamon
½ tsp.	salt (optional)
3 C.	oatmeal
	dash of vanilla (after removing from heat)

Simmer above ingredients before adding oatmeal. Adjust ingredients according to batch size. For the faint of heart, disguise with fruit compote, applesauce, honey or brown sugar, as desired.

FRUIT COMPOTE

2	apples, cut in chunks
1	pear, cut in chunks (canned is OK)
½ C.	raisins
1	banana, cut in chunks
½ C.	sliced rhubarb (if available) or
¼ C	dried cranberries.
	vanilla & honey to taste

Place fruit in saucepan with water at half level of fruit. Simmer until fruit is partially softened, but still shapely. Add vanilla after removing from heat and sweeten with honey as desired. This recipe is good for using up overripe fruit! Also excellent as topping on ice cream, cake or yogurt.

ROCK CHICKENS

Once upon a time, a hunter and guide took to the woods for to partake in their daily hunting rituals. The hunter, possessing something of an appreciation for nature, espied a blue grouse. With a kind of breathy excitement, the Hunter pointed it out to his guide, John Fellow.

I can just hear them now:

HUNTER: *"Hey LOOK, it's a Blue Grouse!"*

JOHN FELLOW: *"YYEeessss, it's a Blue Grouse!"*

John Fellow, a local resident and long time outfitter, had long since moved beyond the natural mystery of the indigent blue grouse. I might add that the grouse is otherwise known as the "Fools Chicken" because it is far too stupid to run. John Fellow, being no fool himself, was eyeing tonight's appetizer, and with a handful of pebbles he was in <u>hot</u> <u>pursuit</u>!

Mental Note: Never taunt John Fellow.

Following a respectable battle, John Fellow returned to camp that evening with something extra special for dinner. Scrawny little thing, but it sure tasted good. We have since dubbed this fowl "The Rock Chicken," and for all of you hunters who have not had due success in the hunt, maybe you have been using the wrong ammo!

PERFECT ROCK CHICKEN

Surely, there is more than one way to cook a Rock Chicken. This is my particular method, suitable for partridge, grouse and other wild fowl. Modify as you please.

1	Rock Chicken, defeathered, deboned, cut into strips (Be sure to remove the stupid part before cooking.)
	olive oil
half clove	garlic, crushed/minced
dash	thyme and/or basil
	pepper
	salt
½ tsp.	grated orange rind (optional)
	or a couple teaspoons of orange juice (optional)

Preheat oil and garlic in skillet. Add strips of meat, coat with spices and sauté uncovered on medium heat until golden brown on one side.

Turn strips over and cover for second half of cooking time. This will help keep it tender. Ready when browned and meat pulls apart easily.

Serve with your best beer.

MOONLIGHT ESCAPADES AT THE SPRING

Having alluded to
the single most coveted extrava-
gance of Chuck's lower camp, let us ex-
pand on the topic. The Bath Tent is situated a ways from camp, with aromatic
pines to the West and a pleasant view up the aspen foothills to the north. It is
a modest white canvas tent that might have seemed lackluster placed next to
the marble baths of Rome — but here on the Middle Piney Creek in the Commissary Range of Wyoming it is a quaint and homey bit of paradise. Especially
for an exhausted, cold and grimy hunter looking to soothe his saddle sores,
and lay out his prayers for the next rousting day of the hunt.

My chore was to fill the barrel reservoir using water piped in from the spring,
and to keep the fire good and stoked for hours so that it would be ready after
dinner. One boiler load of water usually provided three good baths per night.
When the first customer arrived, hot water was diverted into the old-fashioned iron tub and then tempered with cool spring water hauled by hand
from the spring access above. This chore was not made easier by the pre-
dominant slope upon which the whole set up was perched. Nor did the simple
mechanics of the water system improve one's demeanor, as there was a certain trick to dislodging the main feed line to camp, and refitting the temporary line to the boiler without receiving a pointedly cold dowsing in the process. Imagine, if you will, trying to insert a piece of rubber tubing into a

powerful onrush of water? The possibilities are nearly as endless as they are comic, until you get the knack. I was duly motivated to "get the knack." Once the guest was satisfied with the water temperature, I would head back to camp while he enjoyed a good consolatory soak.

One fateful night, the last of the hunters presented himself for his bath. Jay was a soft spoken, soft around the middle kind of fellow from Oregon. I prepared his bath, adjusting the water temperature as directed and then departed as usual. It wasn't until days afterward that I learned what later transpired that night.

Upon stripping down and attempting to submit to the bath, Jay found the water a wee bit hot. So hot in fact that he could not stand to get into it. Frustrated, Jay pulled on his union suit and set out to fill another bucket of cold water from the spring. The bare feet were his first mistake –

I suppose I made it look easy — getting that water from the spring. And I suppose Jay had not payed much attention, seeing as he never figured on having to duplicate the procedure. So our hapless guest was rather unprepared for the full impact of that frigid flume of water that hit him square in the chest as he disconnected the main line. (I am already laughing as I write this) and I expect that the rotating power spray that followed as he tried to reinsert the line was equally exhilarating (now I am really laughing) and I wish to God I had been around to see it. The sojourn back to the bath tent hauling the 5-gallon bucket of water could only have been improved by the slippery trail, moistened from all the traffic before him.

I am not certain if he made it back with that first bucket in tact, or if he had to return to the source for another lesson. And one can only speculate as to how many other unfortunate hunters have befallen this fate on some snowy winter night. But in mind's eye, I can see him squealing and cussing in the moonlight like the Pillsbury Doughboy on a bad acid trip – a most comical sight.

ELK PEPPER STEAK*

Poor Jay — only excitement he got that year was the moon-light escapade at the spring. He never did get his elk. The least we could do is taunt him to come back and try again with this nice recipe.

1 lb.	elk sirloin
1 C.	bell pepper, sliced
1	red onion, sliced
1-8oz pkg.	fresh mushrooms
1 clove	fresh garlic
1 T.	soy sauce
½ tsp.	salt
2 T.	olive oil

Cut the sirloin into strips. Heat olive oil in a skillet; add garlic, soy sauce, onion, and elk. Sauté until browned. Add remaining ingredients and simmer, covered until vegetables are tender, stirring occasionally.

Steamed wild rice, scallop potatoes, fresh green salad are excellent compliments for this entree.

*Bagged from Dennis Fisher's Wild Game Recipes, where it is featured as his best recipe for cooking elk or venison as the peppers seem to take away all unwanted wild taste. www.fishersnet.com Copyright ©1995, 1996, 1997, 1998 by Dennis Fisher.

COOKIE BAGS A DEER

huh?.

Since it appears I am ratting on everyone else, it is only fair to fess up about myself. Especially since I know a few guys who would holler if I didn't, and if anyone happened to be any good at drawing cartoons, I would be in real trouble.

It was a long tedious drive to and from Jackson, Wyoming via Big Piney. And a hundred miles each way seems especially long when there are endless stretches of monotonous prairie, and you are particularly sleep-deprived. With the last hunter packed off for home, we were attempting the drive in that post-season exhaustion that the likes of an outfitter knows very well. A hunter visits for five, maybe 10 days tops. An outfitter has to last several months without a break. It is his most profitable time of the season and his whole winter reserves depend upon it.

So we are driving along, Chuck is trying to keep his eyes open by smoking a cigar, which nearly finishes me. Finally he relinquishes the wheel and succumbes to sleep. This changing of the guard did nothing to improve our chances of arriving safely, because I too was exhausted. It was to be a short and rudely concluded nap.

I was keeping it between the lines fairly well when a cute little deer wandered straight into the highway. For a fleeting second I considered swerving the top-heavy van, which is basically a box on wheels. But then I might not be around to be writing this today. So brace yourself — BONK! I hit the deer.

Sure as shootin' and a lot quicker than any of those hunters got their fool trophies, I bagged a deer without even wasting a bullet.

Chuck was now QUITE awake. (JEEZus!) Bambi was now hamburger, skidding along on the side of the road. I was simply mortified. In all the years of driving, I'd never hit an animal, and I especially loved deer — they are such gentle creatures.

Now steam was gushing from the radiator and I was hoping for an out of body experience. Nothing doing. The ordeal was yet to begin — we still had 60 miles to go and it was damn cold that November night in Wyoming. Please know that on the open plains there is precious little to stop the wind, and in the wintertime it is a bitter wind that howls never ending .

We stopped at every creek from there to Big Piney and prayed luck would hold long enough to get us to the ranch. Each time the distance between overheatings grew shorter, and in direct proportion, the creeks became harder to come by. Chuck could have flagged down help several times, but didn't want to bother anyone. More likely, the life of a game warden is fraught with past offenders who harbor hard feelings for getting caught with their hands in the proverbial cookie jar. Several hours later, I was ripe for bothering just about ANYONE. The night was cold and the van was fading fast, and I finally cajoled Chuck into letting me stop at someone's trailer for water. He agreed but only if I did the knocking, <u>and</u> the talking. Apparently, this was the home of a past offender. Chuck hid in the van.

Hours later, we pulled into the ranch and I hoped that tomorrow I might wake to find this was only a dream. Just a little dream. Bad enough that I had hit a deer, but I hit it smack in the middle and with Chuck's van and you could see the perfect imprint of Bambi in the radiator grill. Chuck was kind enough not to tease me, though he did let slip a few remarks about my perfect aim now and then. In ways the silence was worse. I figured he must be really pissed.

Hunting guide Mike later remarked how they ought to get me a gun so's maybe I could shoot a few rounds in practice for next hunting season. I smiled sweetly and asked, *"Would he like to play target?"* There were no more smart remarks about my per-   fect aim.

Mike Playing Target

Though I survived the ordeal, it was to be one of the more humiliating moments of my short-lived "career" and I have always felt terrible about damaging Chuck's van. Out there, the vehicle is a most important piece of equipment, and it is a long sorry haul without one. I imagine it was a long while before Chuck handed over his keys to the hired help — and even longer before he ventured to take a road nap!

LBJ'S FAVORITE VENISON CHILI*

2 T.	vegetable oil
3 lbs.	venison, cubed (may substitute hamburger, be sure to drain the excess grease)
2 cloves	garlic, finely chopped
2 med.	onions, chopped
6 tsp.	New Mexican red chili powder (or your favorite brand)
3 cans	Lone Star Beer (Permission to use your favorite beer also. Recipe calls for 2 beers, the extra is for you to drink while making the chili!)
2	green chilies, chopped
1 tsp.	oregano
1 tsp.	ground cumin
2-16 oz. cans	stewed tomatoes (diced)
	salt to taste

Combine venison (hamburger), oil if using venison, onions and garlic in a skillet and sear until the meat is lightly browned.

Transfer this mixture to a large pot, add the remaining ingredients, and bring to a boil. Reduce the heat and simmer for 1 hour. Stir frequently with wooden spoon. (*If spoon catches fire, the chili is ready!*)

LBJ liked it without beans (I guess you could add beans if you liked, after all, it is your chili.) accompanied by a glass of milk, and saltine crackers.

Extra hot additions if desired: add 2 chopped red chili pods or 2 Jalapeno peppers.

*This recipe included with permission (along with a few dashes of humor) from Mason Gray's ww.firegirl.com. Check it out!

VENISON SUMMER SAUSAGE*

5 lb.	hamburger or venison mixed with beef tallow
6 tsp.	curing salt (or pickling salt)
2½ tsp.	mustard seed
2½ tsp.	coarse ground pepper
2½ tsp.	garlic salt (3 cloves of garlic chopped can also be used)
1 tsp.	hickory smoke salt (Some liquid smoke may be used)

First day: Mix in a large bowl, cover and refrigerate.

Second day: Mix again and refrigerate.

Third day: Leave in refrigerator and do not stir.

Fourth day: Form into 5 rolls. Place on broiler pan and rack. Place on lower rack of oven. Bake 8 hours at 160 - 170°F degrees. Turn occasionally.

Refrigerate or keep in freezer.

*This is Dennis Fisher's favorite sausage recipe, featured at www.fishersnet.com . It takes four days to complete a batch but well worth the wait. Sent to him from Bruce Powers who lives in Texarkana, Arkansas. Copyright ©1995, 1996, 1997, 1998 by Dennis Fisher.

A LITTLE LOCAL COLOR

Here is a little local color as retold by Mike the hunting guide. Please keep in mind that people get a little eccentric out there in the prairie, though I am told this woman was actually a transplant resident – maybe Wyoming is not entirely to blame. Still, I have heard some WILD stories about Wyoming people in general, and I am convinced, it must be something in the wind.

Anyways, a certain local girl named Tink attended a Halloween party naked, and wrapped in cellophane. As you can imagine, the local boys afforded her a wide berth. It would not be good, no, not good at all, for the wife to catch him fraternizing with a cellophane-wrapped woman. Many nights of sleeping in the truck would soon follow. Gossip has it that one of the boys finally dared to venture near the brazen thing and talked a bit until she coquettishly mused that *it was too bad he hadn't come naked and on roller skates...* Puzzled, he asked why? She quipped, *"Cause you coulda' been my pull toy."* I had to admire the spunk of that girl, and I bet that fellow blushed from here to Idaho.

Sometime after hearing this story, I was helping Chuck tow his demolished van (post-Bambi incident) to the mechanic's house. I was to drive the truck with Chuck navigating the van in tow. Chuck offered that maybe now he could be MY pull toy!

"NOPE, I don't think you're quite dressed the part Chuck!"

Talk about a little "local color!"

PECOS "RED" STEW*

2 lbs.	boneless pork butt, cut into large chunks (1½")
2 T.	olive oil
2 C.	onion, chopped
1 C.	green pepper, chopped
	or 1-8 oz. can of chopped green chilies
2	cloves garlic, minced
¼ C.	fresh cilantro, chopped
3-4 T.	chili powder
2 tsp.	oregano
1 tsp.	salt
1 tsp.	crushed red pepper
2-8 oz.	cans chicken broth (low fat/low sodium if possible)
3 C.	potatoes, peeled & 1" cubed
2 C.	fresh or frozen kernel corn
1-16 oz.can	garbanzo beans

Heat oil in Dutch oven. Brown pork over medium-high heat. Stir in onions, green pepper, garlic, cilantro, chili powder, oregano, salt, red pepper and chicken broth. Cover; cook over medium-low heat for 45-55 minutes or until pork is tender. Add potatoes, corn and beans. Cover; cook 15-20 minutes longer. Serves 8.

*Smithfield Lean Generation Pork Recipe.

CHILI CHEESE CORNBREAD

1½ C.	yellow corn meal
1 C.	sour cream
2/3 C.	corn oil
16 oz. can	cream style corn
2	eggs
7 oz. can	chopped green chilies
1 T.	butter
8 oz.	sharp cheddar cheese, grated

Preheat oven to 350°F. Mix all ingredients except cheese. Spread butter in 9 x 14 inch baking pan (or substitute cooking oil spray). Pour half of the mixture into dish and sprinkle half of cheese over mixture. Pour remaining mixture into dish and top with cheese. Bake for 45-50 minutes.

THE HEART ROCKS

I have a little secret.

I do not drink or smoke or chew, or tell rude cowboy jokes (well not often) and I do not lie or spin tall tales without some foundation of truth. I'm not running from the law and I have never been a man. But I do find a certain fascination with rocks – in the shape of hearts.

One day I pulled off the highway, just north of Thermopolis, Wyoming to make a first attempt at painting the red rock landscape. Later, I walked down the hill to one of the red bluffs – wanting to see what that redness looked like up close, what it felt like in my hand. As it happened, the first piece I picked up was in the perfect shape of a heart. I have been finding them ever since.

Yes, heart rocks up and down the Continental Divide, in every shape, color and size – but still in the unmistakable shape of a heart. I believed this to be a message from above. What else would it be?

In 1993 I had driven away from Maine seeking a life I could love, not merely survive. Within weeks, I found that first heart rock. The trip that followed, which lasted four years, was sometimes difficult. Most times it was magical. But always I followed my heart, and it seemed that whenever my courage wavered, I found a heart rock or two to boost it along. Most usually when I least expected it.

Taking such a profound leap of faith is not often easy, but sometimes it is necessary. When the need becomes greater than the fear, it is surprising what we can accomplish. And I am thankful for every reminder along the way, no matter how small. An angel might as well have left those heart rocks as far as I was concerned, for they were precious stepping stones to find the way. I have shared many a heart rock with friends who might have needed a lift too, as I believe hearts are intended to be shared. (Damn good thing, or the car'd be down on its axles.)

Chuck Thornton is a decent guy who seemed somewhat amused with this heart rock thing at first. Probably because he had never met anyone so strange, and he was too polite to make fun of me. Admittedly, I am a bit different from the average woman in those parts, which occasionally caused me to become the topic of speculation. One hunter, after hearing of my wandering lifestyle, became convinced that I was "a'runnin from the law." He would have bet his dimwitted life on it. Must have been one of those suspicious types who did not approve independent women on the loose.

Anyway, too much of a good thing can become a nuisance, and eventually, I became as much with my heart rocks. Realizing this, I kept it to myself. It did not help that Chuck's part of the country was just chock full of heart rocks – big and small. If you had seen that land, you would understand. You might even take a few home for yourself – and I highly recommend that you do. Some gifts can only be found by taking extraordinary measures, by doing something new, or by taking a closer look at something you would normally pass by. Think – how many beautiful things in life we all pass by, without ever noticing?

As the season wound down, Chuck and his hunters surprised me with a gesture of how much they appreciated my cooking and presence in their hunting camp. Some even confided that I had been their lucky omen. One day they returned to tell of a special place near Darby Mountain itself. A natural spring … in the shape of a heart. They decided to name it after me. This may have been somewhat tongue-in-cheek, but I was touched all the same.

It was not long before hunting season came to its close. All the equipment was packed out on a prayer and winter came in full force soon after. I never was able to take a horse and ride up to the spring. But somewhere in the Commissary Range of Wyoming is a quiet place that bears my name, and no matter what you might think about rocks and things in the shape of a heart, there is something pretty special about that.

Thanks guys.

GRANDMA BECK'S SPONGE CAKE*

The very best cooking often transcends mere ingredients and measures, and the best cooks always seem to have one secret ingredient in common — they cook with love.

Grandma Beck was a woman of the heart and all that love flowed into her delicious cooking like sunlight. As a young child, Granddaughter Becky recalls that whenever she was sick, Grandma Beck promised to make this special cake as soon as she was well enough to eat. Amazing how fast a child will recover when such loving treats await them. Grandma Beck was a smart lady, and this is her coveted Sponge Cake recipe.

8	eggs (medium)
2	lemons (juice & rinds)
2 C.	sugar
1 C.	flour

Separate eggs yolks from whites. Beat yolks and sugar until smooth. Add juice from lemons plus 1 tablespoon of rind, or more if you like. Add flour to this mixture.

In a separate bowl, beat egg whites until stiff. Fold small amount of flour/egg yolk mixutre into whites, then gently fold whites into remaining flour/egg yolk mixture.

Pour into a buttered 9 x 13 pan and bake at 300°F for 50-60 minutes. Cake should have sort of a hard crust on top and a moist lemony bottom. The longer the cake sits after baking, the better it is.

Cut into squares and serve.

*Recipe from Becky Culpepper, who remembers Grandma Beck most fondly.

CHAPTER II

The Mystery of Coulter Lake

MY BRIEF FLING WITH COULTER LAKE

Imagine that you are standing in a kitchen at a guest ranch perched by a small lake, tucked away in the cradle of a mountain range high above a little town called Rifle, Colorado. Now imagine that you have left your one escape (the car) parked several miles down the mountain and actually consented to travel by snow machine to this ranch with all your earthly possessions in tow. Getting nervous? The kitchen is small, but features a big shiny cook stove and loads of culinary equipment. The spice selection is even decent. And out every window is a lovely view of the mountain slopes, the lake, or tall aspen groves peaceful and white, and there are winding trails promising of more breathtaking views, should anyone have a mind to follow them. I say "anyone" because as the new cook, it is not likely to be you. Not often anyway. Say howdy to your new home. No, you are not dreaming, though many times later you will wish you were.

I was hired at Coulter Lake mostly by way of phone personality. Truthfully, my humor was the best thing I had to offer, that soon fizzled once I got an eyeful of what I had gotten into. The owner of Coulter Lake thought I sounded fairly promising over the phone, and yes, I did know how to make food taste good. I have since learned to hold back on some of the charm since there is no substitute for experience, and personality alone rarely gets the job done.

Standing in this kitchen I could not have imagined all of what was to come. I soon realized how much being chained to a kitchen for days on end was akin to hell. Nonetheless, I dug in and did my best since they had my word on it, and I only cried once.

Coulter Lake Guest Ranch began as a homestead back in the early 1900's, evolving into a hunting camp with cabins on the lake for summer guests. The ranch was then purchased by some folks from California, I will call them the Coulters —who apparently thought it would be a nice retirement hobby. The Coulters actively operated the ranch until 1997, when it was sold to the next generation of new blood. At which point, I imagine they crawled away while they still had the strength.

If charm and comfort are what you seek, Coulter Lake Guest Ranch has tons of it. I could see it all from my little hellhole. A beautiful rustic lodge complete with a hand-hewn pine, family-style dining room, and a lovely big fireplace with a piano, should you care to strike up a tune. Cozy little guest cottages dotted the slope behind the lodge and down along the lake. I imagined how dreamy it must be in the summertime, though I had already oathed a promise to escape long before the first bud. The only thing that could possibly make this job more hellish was the prospect of a hot summer, in a hotter kitchen, in Western garb — all of which were *status quo* during the summer season. My feet hurt just thinking about the prospect of cooking in cowboy boots.

During summer, the ranch is crawling with wranglers and staff; all decked out in Western chic and Roy Rogers smiles, ready to cater your every whim. Coulter Lake offers trail rides, sing-a-longs, cookouts and various daily activities to keep the family amused. For the extra adventurous, try a whitewater expedition on the Colorado River, followed by a soothing soak in the Glenwood Hot Spring or a meditative hour in the vapor caves (massage optional). These activities are apart from the ranch, but easily obtainable. Summer guests stay for a minimum of a week.

During winter, rates go down as the snow piles high. Coulter Lake becomes a snowmobile lodge promising of good food, hot cocoa and a warm inviting fire and there is no minimum stay requirement. Bring your own night-cap. I remember looking out the windows as the snow came down in chunks and thinking *it could snow all it wanted because I didn't have to commute anywhere!* One day the Coulters took the crew snowmobiling up on the mesa top, which was about 10,000 feet in elevation. The snow was fresh powder, probably seven or more feet deep, and the view was endless. I still have pictures, and fortunately, the frostbite was not permanent.

Every once in a while, a snowmobiler would get lost or hung up on the mountain somewhere and they would call in the troops. The emergency search team from the valley below was impressive, manned with local people who were well acquainted with the perils of the high country — seasoned snowmobilers with years of experience.

Coulter Lake boasts of a spring fed, man-made, trout-stocked lake, on which you may try your hand at fishing. If you ask real nice, they might even cook one up for you, but mainly, it is catch and release. That winter, we had one fellow who was contented to sit by his rig on the ice and haul in fish. He asked if he could take some home (pretty please) to which we agreed. Sometime later we realized the fool had caught quite a bundle and that maybe we had better cut him off. I wonder if he made it all the way home before the little fishies thawed out?

Personally, the 20-mile excursion from Rifle to the ranch was worth investigating in of itself. Rifle Gap is a long winding canyon, which narrows as the elevation increases, offering many scenic jewels to discover along the way. The eccentric artist Christo, who liked to wrap large parcels of land (and even islands) in pink canvas, once became enamored with Rifle Gap and wrapped <u>it</u> in pink. They named a puny camping area after him.

During the summer, the Gap is a rock fanatic's dream, attracting climbers from all parts of the world. During winter, it features vast walls of ice which climbers are wont to challenge. For those who prefer to keep their feet on the ground, the Gap beholds luminous blue ice caves, which you may explore in wonder. Along the way you may enjoy a visit to Rifle Falls, an enchanted cascade featuring winding foot trails through a virtual fairyland.

Campers may choose from any number of campsites for a nominal fee. And of course, Rifle Creek is the lifeblood of the valley running through it.

Get your paperwork in order and you can fish this inviting creek, or even the Reservoir below. The Gap also boasts a fish hatchery, which I believe regularly stocks the creek, so you might anticipate some action.

For hikers there are multitudes of challenging trails. For the Nordic skier or snowshoer, a limitless white wonderland with groomed trails and fresh powder to explore. You'll make great sport for the Mountain Lions.

Important Note: Snowmobilers from lower elevations, be certain to have your jets adjusted for the highlands (8,000 - 10,000 ft). I have seen vacations ruined for this small but important detail. Also, consider how well YOU might handle high elevations. Drink lots of water, get plenty of sleep, and be mindful of headaches or nosebleeds. These are symptoms of elevation sickness.

My favorite pastime was to snowmobile down to the trailhead on my day off, drive 30 miles to Glenwood Springs and disappear into the hot spring vapor caves for a soothing meditation. This was the single most relaxing bit of solitude I could find and it was my one saving sanity for the week to come. One evening, as I snowmobiled back to the ranch in the dark, four elk leapt across the trail in my headlight — an image so haunting and surreal that it remains with me to this day. I remember thinking *wow, is this really my life?* Have you ever done that? Caught yourself at some odd moment and realized that this was really your life? For a second I could not imagine how I ever came to be in this place so far from my native land. I knew it was not my home and that I would not stay long, but there were many gifts during the time I did stay.

Another favorite pastime was to take advantage of short breaks in the workday and walk the snowmobile trail toward the mesa tops. I would bring my cedar flute and play wistful songs, breathing in the solitude as the notes echoed off the canyon walls. Without fail, my footsteps in the snow were much clearer upon returning to the ranch, than the ones departing. Often, a small flock of chickadees would follow, calling and playing overhead. I returned their greetings and enjoyed their lighthearted company. One day a raven called from far across the valley, coming closer until he was turning a figure eight pattern overhead. I had mastered a fair imitation of a raven's call during the many sojourns in the hills, and I managed to hold his curiosity for some time — yet another welcomed if not curious visitation.

One day, while retracing my tracks from a previous afternoon's wanderings, I found that a mountain lion had followed, leaving *sign* where I had lingered at a favorite meditation spot. I imagine she had watched me often, though I never saw her. I have heard that when such an animal steps into your tracks, it is an invitation to know them. The mountain lion is aptly nicknamed the *ghost cat*.

As spring beckoned and winter business dropped off, I set about exploring elk runs on the high slopes behind the ranch. These were the elk's winter hiding places, tangled scrub oak thickets and deep hilly crags. The network of trails were fascinating and the scent of elk was thick as the winter buildup of elk doo doo.

For the most part, I had not found anybody I could relate to at this job and found it lonely. The guests were often delightful, though fleeting in my world, and I rarely had time to visit with them. Mostly it was the quiet moments out of doors, and the curious creatures that came to visit who were my friends. Mrs.C. was convinced I had a touch of "attention deficit disorder " — how disappointingly typical of her, such labeling tendency being a school teacher affliction. My heart just was not in the kitchen and the life of a ranch cook did not wear well on me. I became exhausted and unable to sleep. Maintain focus? At times, I could barely maintain standing position. Besides, Mrs. C. was a control freak and was slowly driving me insane. I had this image of her holding the ranch together so determinedly that if an earthquake were to level the <u>entire</u> <u>mountain</u>, she would manage to keep the ranch in tact! Read on and see what that woman could do with her vocal cords!

Ranch cooking is a challenge, even to far more experienced cooks than my-self. I've heard stories …and I could tell you a few. Worse yet, during the winter season all those helpful summer staff people migrate to warmer climes, so I had NO backup, which nicely accompanied NO EXPERIENCE. When I developed bronchitis I worked straight through it, still cooking three meals a day (no rest for the wretched) and trying to hold my act together. When Christmas and New Years rolled around my family was 3,000 miles away, and I was cooking the traditional holiday menu – for 30 guests. Though I knew this was part of the job, it still felt weird. But I did my best to persevere and learn, and I prayed my cooking was edible.

In this time I learned that the distinction between *isolation* and *solitude* was mainly how you viewed it, and how you used your time. I also realized that *the chains that bind us best are the ones we choose ourselves*. (If you don't like Hell, why do you keep choosing it?) In spite of this lofty wisdom, I continued cooking for several more seasons, as I incorrectly assumed that it was the *indoor* hell that disagreed with me so. Foolishly, the next season I opted for the outdoor variety. I will admit, there is a fine line between courage and stupidity.

March 29th of 1995 was the last time I saw Coulter Lake Guest Ranch (except in my nightmares). Mr. & Mrs. C. graciously allowed me to depart early since winter was on the decline, and quite possibly, I was driving them bonkers. At this point, the ranch had no bookings and I was counting the days… The 29th was also my birthday and I could not imagine a BETTER gift. As a parting gesture, Mrs. C. presented me with a copy of *The Dude Ranch Cookbook*, "*in memory of having braved Coulter Lake Guest Ranch!! Happy Days of cooking ahead!*" I was touched, especially since I had coveted that book all winter long. I will assume that last part about *happy cooking* was purely in jest.

For years after, I imagine they just shook their heads at the mention of my name, saying, "*poor Deborah, I hope she recovered …*" or maybe, "*gee, I hope we didn't break her for good …*" and "*wasn't she a funny thing?*"

But you know – nobody made me choose that job. There was no ball and chain in that kitchen – it was in my mind and I simply was not cut out for this kind of life. I have since decided that the best way to experience a guest ranch or outfitter is to be a guest, and from now on, I intend to prove it!

CHILI CHEESE OMELET*

10	eggs
½ C.	flour
1 T.	baking powder
½ tsp	salt
1 lb.	Monterey Jack cheese
2 C.	small curd cottage cheese
½ C.	salad oil
2-4 oz. cans	diced green chilies

Beat eggs; add flour, baking powder, salt and blend. Add cheese and oil, mix and add green chilies.

Pour into 13 x 9 greased pan and bake at 350°F for 45-50 minutes.

Serve with a side of green or red salsa.

* Both of these recipes are long-time favorites at Coulter Lake Guest Ranch.

ORGASMIC CINNAMON ROLLS

2 pkgs.	active dry yeast
2 C.	warm water
½ C.	sugar
2 tsp.	salt
¼ C.	vegetable oil
1	egg
7 C.	flour
	melted butter
	cinnamon & sugar
	confectioner's sugar
	orange juice

In a large glass bowl, dissolve warm water, yeast and sugar (do not use metal utensils). Set this bowl inside a larger bowl or pan containing warm water and allow a few minutes to activate yeast.

Mix in salt, oil and egg. Add flour several cups at a time and mix well (may use electric mixer). Do not knead. Place dough in a greased bowl and cover with waxed paper and a damp cloth. Dough may be kept in refrigerator for several days until ready to use, or left at room temperature to rise for immediate use.

Once dough has risen, roll out on a floured surface using greased rolling pin. Brush with melted butter then sprinkle with cinnamon and sugar. Roll up dough and cut it approx. 1 inch thick (or to desired size). Arrange rolls on baking sheet 1-2 inches apart for "break apart" rolls, cover and let rise in warm place until desired size. Bake at 400°F until golden brown, approx. 12-15 minutes. Glaze with mixture of confectioner's sugar and orange juice (just thick enough to drizzle) and serve warm.

For variations: Add chopped apple or raisins to the cinnamon & sugar layer prior to rolling dough. Makes 15 large, or 30 small rolls. For doubled batches, divide dough to roll out in small quantity.

YOO HOOOooooooooooooooo

Yoo HOO? Indeed, a time-honored tradition at Coulter Lake Guest Ranch — fifty plus years in the running. They have tried bells and chimes and hollering till the gills turn blue, but nothing works like the old Yoo Hoo. One good yell and the half the mountain will know it is dinnertime, especially given the natural acoustics, which amplifies it nicely.

Yoo Hoo is a must for any ranch cook wannabee (probably why I will shun such jobs in the future), and it is a practice borne purely out of frustration and the need for release? YOU try cooking for 14 hours a day and see if you don't feel like hollering!

However, Yoo Hoo was never my strong point as I was just a little too shy for such public displays. Besides I could never have hoped to equal the talents of Mrs. Coulter, omnipotent Yoo Hooer at Coulter Lake. Do not let her petite demeanor fool you – she has got a set of pipes that will send you to running for the fine crystal. Hers is a Yoo Hoo to be admired, and not for the faint of heart.

Miss Page (former wrangler) discovered this one night when she and a few wranglers retired (with ample liquor) to the far side of Coulter Lake (which in my book measured more like a pond) for a wee nip. As is often the case, alcohol amplifies any good time, and soon Mrs. C. was to don housecoat and trudge to said pond. The forthcoming Yoo Hoo was intended to rally the group to come to their senses. Mrs. C., a retired but not recovered school-teacher, did not expect to hear it returned back to her in a less than respect-able manner. Especially not by her prized and normally upstanding female wrangler. One can only imagine what bits of wisdom were passed that night, suffice to say it only happened once. NEVER — underestimate the power of the Yoo Hoo.

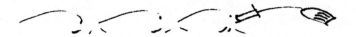

One morning, Matt the Wrangler suggested that Mr. C. ought to take a crack at the Yoo Hoo? Mr. C. matter of factly replied that he did not believe he could match his wife's expertise. Matt offered that with the help of a certain pair of pliers, Mr. C. might be surprised.

LORD CHARLEY'S CORN CHOWDER*

Since I considered the whole Yoo Hoo thing rather corny, which it was, and since Mrs. C. herself did bestow this recipe upon me, it seems fitting to include it at this time.

½ C.	onion, chopped
½ C.	celery, chopped
¼ C.	green pepper, chopped
1/3 C.	bacon, chopped

Brown in skillet and add the following:

1¼ qt.	chicken stock
1 tsp.	salt
¼ tsp.	ground white pepper
½ tsp.	thyme
1 lb.	potatoes, peeled & diced
15 oz.	frozen cut corn

Simmer one half hour.

In separate pan melt 2 oz. butter, add 1 T. flour, then 1 qt. of Half & Half. Whip smooth and add to soup. Cook 10 minutes to blend.

May garnish with crumbled bacon.

*Recipe from the legendary Lord Charley's restaurant!

SNOWMOBILING FUN WITH SKEETER

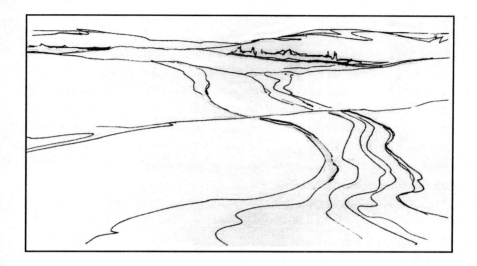

One beautiful Sunday, The Coulters generously offered to take the crew snowmobiling up to the mesa tops. This was a rare, one-time event and we were all excited. With over two feet of fresh snow, the mesa, which hangs at about 10,000 ft in elevation, would be a pristine winterland. I packed my camera for the ride.

Now even though I grew up in a winter recreation area, I had never done any serious riding, especially not in deep powder, and so considered myself basically inexperienced. Fortunately, I was allotted the one long-track machine they owned. A "long-track" will stay up on powder when other machines get bogged down. Even so, it was a trip I would not forgot.

First off, the wimpiest machine died halfway up the mountain. With solemn pronouncements uttered, we paired up and continued on up the hill. Oh it was glorious — the sun was bright, the air clear and the snow like endless white velvet. Once on top, we cut loose and zoomed around the gentle slopes. You might think you could fly off the edge of the world, but there was no discernable end to it. Of course, we had our momentary wrecks, which at the beginning were mostly my doing. I was timid, still getting the knack of shifting one's butt rapidly as the snow shifted beneath my machine. A sluggish butt meant <u>wipe out!</u> But I caught on and soon the title of Person Most Likely to Cause Wipeout went to the handyman, Skeeter.

Now Skeeter was an interesting case. A kindhearted, Neanderthal redneck sort of guy from Grand Junction, Colorado whose genuine native accent mangled the simplest of words like "wash." He pronounced it "<u>worrush</u>!" Skeeter liked to imagine himself living out his golden years in a small wooded cabin, a virtual hermit with only a few comforts, which would certainly include a shotgun. The shotgun was mainly for anyone fool enough to trespass (unless it was a pretty young thing) and besides, it fit with the image. Skeeter would be as crotchety as his ole Grandpa and mean as a junkyard dog. Unfortunately, Skeeter was a teddy bear at heart. Better he acquire a tape recording of a junkyard dog, which he could play in the event of vagrants come sniffing around.

Skeeter had grown up during the sixties when it would be fair to speculate that he had smoked his share of weed, drank his share of hooch, and smacked his head on more than his share of rocks. Skeeter had been rattling around the mountains all his life and it was quite evident that he had some wear and tear on him as he was <u>NOT</u> exactly the sharpest knife in the drawer.

Skeeter would burst into the kitchen flushed and grimy with snow and sweat, hair filthy and filled with dirt from some horrid job under the lodge and bawl **"Ah'm HUnnNGRAY! Ah'm TIRED! Wwwwhere's my DINNER!"** as he sashayed his grimy self toward the stove, heaving and dripping melted snow and who knew what all else? Guests would look up and wonder what all the cat had drug in, and why it was near their food? I would quickly hustle Skeeter out, but he would be right back at it  the next night. As slow as Skeeter was about some things, he was quick to take insult, and so any comment about his presence near the food was taken with the highest offense. One day, at my whit's end, I decided to outdo Skeeter at his own game. Next time he came busting in I bawled *"Ah'mmmm HUN-GRY! Ah'mmmm TIRED! Wwwhere's my DINNER"* in the most comical exaggerated rendition I could muster, repeating it as necessary for about the next week. Apparently, Skeeter did not like the sound of himself in stereo and I never heard a peep out of him again. Now back to the snowmobile adventure.

Skeeter could not seem to catch on to the butt technique. No matter how he tried, he could not shift it fast enough to keep from having a wreck, until I began speculating that his hind area was just plain numb. When Skeeter went down, we ALL went down trying to avoid him, and in that fine, deep powder — the second you were off the machine you were up to your chest in snow. Powder so fine you literally had to SWIM to get back to your machine.

On the outside, it was kind of comical – espe-cially when we were scattered, limp forms in the snow like that "boneless chicken ranch cartoon" by Gary Larson. But hours later it was definitely not funny. We were soaked, ex-hausted — and lost. All that new snow had rendered the last section of trail invisible, and the grooming contraption had yet to get around. Worse yet, I had made the classic mistake of being poorly dress in leggings and long johns instead of an insulated snowsuit. My wet clothes were beginning to freeze and the sun was heading down.

It was inevitable that they would switch Skeeter off his machine and onto mine. I dutifully took my place on back, genuflecting and muttering. Regardless of his poor operating abilities, Skeeter was still a man and relegating him to the back seat was apparently a last resort as far as some people were concerned. Oh how I suffered. Several swampings later (which resulted in my being planted head first in snow) they finally put Skeeter on the back of Pam's machine. Pam was not only a female, but also she was taller than Skeeter who had his nose visibly out of joint – but by then we were beyond caring. It was decided to abandon the search for the lost trail in favor of retracing the long way back to the lodge. Meanwhile, I was nearly at the point of hypothermia, which I did not share with the others –I was too busy berating myself for not dressing right and otherwise preoccupied with trying to preserve body heat. The next setback was in the form of a burnt out headlight on Pam and company's machine. Lovely. We sandwiched them between us and made a run for it as I kept my headlight trained just to the right or left, so the trail was lit up ahead. For my kindness, I was rewarded with a perfect view of Skeeter's butt protruding out his low hanging jeans. Indeed, every time they went over a mogul I got mooned.

Yessir, it was a memorable trip back to the ranch that night. The high mountain air cut straight through as we sped into the darkness. I have heard that some Native peoples know how to let the elements pass "through them" without taking their bodyheat — but without the benefit of a lifetime of scout training to call upon, that thought did little to warm me. Honestly, I have never been so cold in all my life. Skeeter caused several more swampings, even from the <u>back</u> end of the snow machine where he was literally dead weight. (I was thinking he was going to be *dead <u>meat</u>* if he caused one more screw up.) About halfway back they ditched the machine again, fumbling and cursing as I watched the rest of the party disappear around the bend. Incensed, I nearly shoved them aside as I climbed atop the machine to neatly right it — with just a bit of motivation I can just about move a mountain.

Meanwhile, back at the ranch, Skeeter retreated to his quarters feeling somewhat emasculated. Actually, skulked would be the word — but my lips were too blue, and my teeth chattering too hard to care and I still had to throw together dinner. Somewhere along the next day I finally got my body heat back, though a few little mementos lingered for weeks afterward. Two perfect red circles of frostbite, one on each kneecap where the wind had battered them raw. Yes, two lovely reminders of the first, and the <u>last</u> time I ever went snowmobiling with Skeeter!

CHILI COLORADO*

Chilly Colorado, that is an understatement! This recipe strikes me as a good warm up for such a cold adventure. Had there been a big enough pot, I would have been tempted to crawl into it.

6	dried ancho or pasilla chilies
3 ½ C.	beef broth
3 lb.	boneless beef chuck, cut in ½" cubes
2 T.	vegetable oil
1 lg.	onion, chopped
4 lg.	garlic cloves, crushed and finely chopped
½ tsp.	salt
2 tsp.	ground cumin seed
1 T.	chili powder
1 T.	cornmeal (optional)

Remove stems and seeds from chilies. Coarsely chop chilies and place in bowl, cover with boiling beef broth and let steep for 30 minutes. Heat oil in large Dutch oven, add onion and cook, stirring constantly until soft and lightly browned. Add garlic, salt, and beef cubes. Cook, stirring constantly, just until beef loses its pink color.

Strain chilies, reserving liquid and chilies. Stir 2 ½ cups of chili liquid into beef. Stir in chili powder and ground cumin seed and bring to a boil. Reduce heat and simmer, uncovered over medium-low heat for 1 hour, stirring constantly.

Place soaked chilies and remaining liquid in blender container, cover and blend until smooth. (If necessary, add ½ cup more of water to make blending easier.) Add mixture to beef and cook over medium-low heat, stirring occasionally for 30 minutes or more until meat is tender.

If a thicker chili is desired, gradually stir in cornmeal 1 tablespoon at a time then cook, stirring constantly until mixture is thickened. Taste and season with salt as desired. Remove from heat and ladle into bowls.

Serve with a variety of condiments such as chopped yellow peppers, red onions, tomatoes, avocado, fresh lime or grated cheese. Makes twelve ½ servings.

* Sourced from Arielle's Recipe Archives at http://recipes.alastra.com

TRADITIONAL CORNBREAD

1 C.	flour
¾ C.	yellow corn meal
4 T.	sugar
3 tsp.	baking powder
½ tsp.	salt
1	egg
1 C.	milk
3 T.	butter, melted

Preheat oven to 350°F. Mix flour, corn meal, sugar, baking powder and salt together in a bowl. Pour egg and milk mixture in bowl, beat until well mixed and add melted butter. Beat again. Pour into well-greased pan or cast iron skillet. Bake 40-45 minutes until edges are just brown.

CHAPTER III

The Misery of Shamus Henry

THE NIGHT THE HORSES RUN OFF

Maybe I should not laugh about this, but I do.

My first trip into the hills under the auspices of one Shamus Henry was during early June — rather early to be packing in Wyoming. But Shamus Henry prided himself in being the first <u>fool</u> in, and the last <u>fool</u> out (one of those macho things) so there we were, packing in through 12 miles of mud and snow and fallen trees, which took considerable creativity to circumnavigate with pack animals in tow. The horses were spooky and out of shape. I was green, and out of shape. And the head wrangler Gil Hoss was in some sort of shape, which I couldn't really discern though he insisted it drove women wild. I could, however, surmise that Gil was regretting his decision to return for a second season, as he did nothing but piss and moan from the start.

I will admit that first ride in was a trip to remember. Normally tranquil summer trails wore their ugly spring faces, featuring large mud holes, which have been known to swallow horses, and nearly did; slick, icy bridges and flooded creeks to cross; and snow, which was still up to the horses bellies in places. Can you feature setting up camp in this muck?

That afternoon, we did arrive at our designated spot on the hill, just in time to chop last year's center poles out of the ice and snow in order to raise the cooking shelter, and set up our own sorry tents in the barely thawed ground and suffer many a cold wet night thereafter. Shamus Henry may have been sleeping in his own warm bed, but technically he was first into the hills, which is all that mattered. It was not long before I noticed an underlying theme to this job.

One night, as Gil was completing his chores, I announced that his elk steak dinner was nearly ready. With the prospect of food, Gil decided to wait on putting the horses out to pasture until he filled his own belly. This was not a good idea. The horses, currently residing in a small, temporary electric corral, were hungry. Being spring, there was almost no feed available to them and Shamus Henry was too stingy to send in packs of alfalfa cubes. After a few nights the horses were restless and angry. I could hear them bickering and banging around the corral, and I had a powerful feeling that the insult of Gil sitting down to a meal might be the last straw. I even said so.

Just as Gil was poised for the first bite, there was a clattering of hooves. Yup, it was an all-out stampede and I do believe the last one farted as it frolicked happily off. Gil's mouth dropped about to his plate. In fact, I believe he could have shoved the whole darned thing in there (along with a half acre of flies) if he'd a mind to. That there was more than just a passel of horses runnin' off — it was the makings of the season's first ass-chewin,' and a good one at that. Gil had a proper panic attack, huffing and puffing and berating himself (Shamus Henry had him well-trained) and likely filling his pants. We strained our eyes to spot up the valley, just on the outside chance they had not run far. I did not let it concern me too much because there was nothing I could do but take care of the cooking end of things. At one point, when Gil finally settled back down to his cold dinner, I hopped up on a fallen log and yelled excitedly, *"Hey looky there Gil —horses!"* Gil was already a'wheeling on his spurs before I could blurt out that I was only joking. Gil did not like that, which was to set the undertone for the rest of the season.

I cannot remember if the horses ran all the way back to the trailhead, but we did catch them eventually, and Gil did get his ass-chewin,' though part of the blame did fairly belong to our lackluster boss, and the ice and snow did continue to melt, making way for greener pastures and contented critters. And we did finally sleep warm and dry at night. But it was not the last time the horses ran off, or the last time Gil got an ass-chewin.

SHOO FLY CAKE

With any luck, here is something that won't run away before you get a chance to eat!

4 C.	all-purpose flour
2 C.	brown sugar
1 C.	butter

Mix above ingredients for crumbs. Reserve 1½ cups of crumb mixture for topping.

2 C.	boiling water
1 C.	molasses
1 T.	baking soda

Pour boiling water, molasses and baking soda into remaining crumbs. Mix well. Pour in a 9 x 12-inch baking pan (ungreased). Bake at 350°F for 45-50 minutes.

Variations

~   A bit of ground ginger will add flavor. Add ¼ tsp. with baking soda.

A LITTLE OFF-TRAIL HUMOR

Shamus Henry will tell you he is a fourth generation Wyoming native, which in those parts is a rather substantial claim if you overlook centuries of native peoples that preceded them. He might also admit that his roots trace back to a certain General of distinction from the Civil War Era. Neither of these facts does anything to improve Shamus Henry's personality. He is as dry as the Wyoming desert, and not nearly as compassionate.

One day Shamus Henry was leading a group of guests on an extended trail ride deep into the Bridger-Teton Wilderness, when he came upon a group of serious backpackers. You would <u>have</u> to be serious to be packing out there because for one thing, it is grizzly country. Backpackers must exercise extreme caution with food and observe strict grizzly regulations. The wise hiker is also sure to make noise or sing when hiking so as not to surprise a bear and unwittingly BECOME food. For this reason, backpackers often attach a bell to their backpacks.

NOTE: There is a long-standing feud between hikers and outfitters. Hikers want horses outlawed because they dig up the trail and outfitters, in return, do not much like tree huggers. <u>Lesson Number One</u>: Do not EVER try to take a horse out from underneath an outfitter.

Anyway, Shamus Henry rides up on the backpackers, who grudgingly step off the trail to allow passage. Shamus Henry pauses and asked the head hiker if he *knows how to tell the difference between grizzly bear shit, and black bear shit?*

The fellow says *No* ——

Shamus Henry says, *"Grizzly bear shit's the one with bells in it."*

The hiker did not smile, crack a grin, or even get angry and commence to cussing. He just stood there expressionless like a bump on a log.

Well what do you know . . . someone finally out-personalitied Shamus Henry.

There is an old bear joke about two fellows out in the woods. All of a sudden a mama bear comes barreling into camp and its clear the men are in danger. The first man kneels down and calmly puts on his running shoes.

The second man screams, "Hey what are you doing that for? You can't outrun a grizzly!" The first man says, " I don't have to outrun the grizzly, I only have to outrun YOU!"

BEAR SHIT   (no-bake squares)

2 C.	sugar
1	stick butter
3 T.	cocoa powder
½ C.	milk

Mix above ingredients in a sauce pan, heat until melted and pour over

3 C.	whole oats
½ C.	peanut butter
1 tsp.	vanilla

Mix and drop in clumps on cookie sheet. Chill until firm. Then eat!
Raisins optional.

*This dessert gratis of Ms. Sandra Hodges, my savior and immediate predecessor at the Root
Ranch. Sandra took no shit, whether it belonged to a bear or otherwise.

DANGED IF THEY DIDN'T RUN OFF AGAIN!

It was around the end of June in the Bridger-Teton Wilderness and since designated wilderness area laws stipulate that you may not exceed 14 consecutive days at each campsite, it was time to move camp. This next move meant crossing the Continental Divide with pack mules and horses in order to access the Atlantic Creek valley on the other side. Being early season, the guys had been scouting the trail and it still did not look good. But our time was up so we packed camp and headed off anyways.

As treacherous as that first trip of the season had been, this second trip (taking us yet another 12 miles further) promised to be even more interesting. Snow, ice, swollen rivers and bottomless mud holes. That year the snow pack had been a record 200% with many mountain passes still 20 to 30 feet under. Crossing rivers would be an extra special event and I could hardly wait.

It was a beautiful, but often harrowing adventure. Eventually, we made our appointed destination in spite of the last crossing, which nearly swallowed a few pack mules and assorted equipment. The mules were quickly relieved of their burdens and all hands set to schlepping a proper camp to order. Meanwhile, I surveyed the disaster that was to become my kitchen for the next two weeks and gritted my teeth. I always found that moment to be over-whelming. Literally a mountain of equipment piled in heaps, the whereabouts of necessary items unknown, and a dozen hungry people wondering when dinner was going to be ready? By the time I finally got camp settled to where I wanted it, the two weeks were up and it was time to pack up again. In the meantime, we were perched on the side of Joy Creek (pronounced "crick") nestled in a valley bordered by Lodge Pole pine forests and I had to admit it was beautiful. The grass was gaining momentum every day and we hoped our horses would remain secure for the night ...

That is, until we were *rudely* awoken to the sound of horses clamoring close our tents. I could hear the lead mare's bell ringing erratically (the lead trouble-maker always wears a bell around its neck so's they can find her when she leads the herd astray) and it did not sound good. Oh Lordy — the horses would not have come into the trees unless they were running from some-thing, probably a bear. Soon the guys were up and yelling, flashlights darting in the darkness and there was mayhem and confusion everywhere. Holy horse puckies Robin, the horses are headed for the creek!

All hands ran down to the water hoping to turn back the herd before they strayed across it. After a good cold mucking about, all hands headed back to bed, tired, wet, and praying with newfound religion that all the horses would be accounted for in the morning. (Ha!) But the next day we were sure enough missing some horseflesh — dismal times indeed, for every pack animal was critically necessary to the grander scheme. I imagine it was liberating for them — being footloose in all that open land. One of the few times a big fat horse can be likened to a needle ... when you are looking for it in big coun-try. Mr. Gil once quipped that I *couldn't find my ass with both hands and a map*. Well just between you and me, I had the same feeling about his lordship just now and I was none too confident about the immediate future. Especially since the next few days were my scheduled time off and a shortage of horses might lead to a personally distasteful conclusion.

Understandably, morale was a little low in camp and I was justifiably edgy. But breakfast had to be prepared as usual and the kitchen put to order.

Fortunately, we had enough stock to pack everyone out, so with the remaining stock saddled and packed, Gil set his face to its best "Mighty Tracker" demeanor and we set off to cross what had become a raging river at the start of our long trek home. I noticed the Mighty Tracker failed to check for fresh horse tracks upon crossing the river. Nonetheless, several miles later the guilty party was spotted — innocently munching grass as if they had not spoiled a good night sleep or nothing. I offered to guard the trail ahead so Gil could round them back toward camp, but Gil's Texas machismo dictated, as lead wrangler, that I remain passively by our guests while he rounded them up. Fine by me — all the better to watch the show.

One of the guests had just inquired how long this would take when the horses rumbled by to the left, followed by the spectacle of Gil tearing after them in hot pursuit. EEEwweee, I had always hoped some Hop-a-long Cassidy type would come along and entertain us. And there he was! Surely this was the finest slapstick comedy for miles and frankly, it was one of my funniest memories of Gil.

Within minutes, the horses stampeded back the other way. Again, Super-Tex was right on their tails. For the next thirty minutes or so we watched the same repeating scenario with comic fascination. Those horses had a whole wide bottomland to run around in, and without a second hand, Gil was helpless to do anything but chase them in circles. But *a man's gotta do what a man's gotta do* (God help him) and in the end the Texan prevailed. Gil spurred the horses back toward camp while we patiently waited, our trusty steeds dozing in the hot midday sun. We were thankful that we would soon be heading out, and the rest of the crew would be happy to see Gil show up with our lost horses, as this meant only a marginal ass-chewin, meaning they would still have something left to sit on.

When Gil returned, there was no mention of his spectacular display of fine Texas horse wrangling. Just a few well deserved snickers. Gil did not like that, which as I mentioned was already the undertone for the season.

WESTERN SCRAMBLED EGGS (seems appropriate)

2 T.	butter
¼ C.	diced bell pepper (red or green)
¼ C.	diced red onion
¼ C.	diced ham or sausage (as available)
8	eggs, lightly beaten
½ C.	grated cheddar cheese
¼ C.	sliced mushrooms
¼ C	water (to add fluffiness to eggs)
1/8 tsp.	salt
1/8 tsp.	pepper

In a large skillet over medium heat, warm the oil. Add the bell pepper and onion; cook until onion is translucent but not browned. Add the ham, eggs, cheese, mushrooms, salt and pepper. Cook, stirring occasionally, until eggs reach desired doneness. Serves 4.

HASH BROWNS

3 T.	olive oil
3 lg.	russet potatoes, baked, cooled, peeled and grated. (Do not overcook!)
dash	seasoned salt
1 tsp.	ground black pepper
½ tsp.	paprika
½ tsp.	ground cumin

In a large pan or griddle, over medium heat, warm oil. Combine remaining ingredients, add to pan and cook, without stirring or otherwise disturbing until potatoes are lightly browned on one side. Flip potato mixture with a spatula and cook until lightly browned on the other side.

AND FRESH SALSA ON THE SIDE

6 med.	tomatoes, diced
1 med.	red onion, diced
1 2"	jalapeno, diced
1 T.	tarragon vinegar
1 lg.	clove garlic, crushed
2	tomatillos, diced
	fresh cilantro & lime

Substitute crushed canned tomato if necessary. Salsa best if made a day or so in advance!

THE WORLD FAMOUS GIL HOSS

Gil Hoss was head boss and second in command at the unforgettable Shamus Henry's outfit in Wyoming. Gil was also a Texan, so naturally his heritage dictated that he make a worthy legend of himself. Admittedly, Gil was quite gifted at the art of storytelling, and had indeed led a very colorful life. Hence, anything he did that was notable (and many a thing that wasn't) was dubbed by his royal lordship as "The World Famous Gil Hoss _____"... go ahead, fill in the blank. The list went on and on. One evening, after the guests had gone to bed, the boys built up the fire so as to burn the daily trash, which was required by law in grizzly country. At the peak moment, Mr. Gil did the honors of throwing the mighty bag onto the fire and missed the mark. Trash slobbered everywhere. I asked politely if this was the "World Famous Gil Hoss Toss?"

Now being head ramrod, Mr. Gil was the obvious first in line for the proverbial ass-chewin' from Shamus Henry. And though it was never severe enough to cripple his abilities in chasing women, the prospect of an ass-chewin' was so distasteful that the fair Mr. Gil lived in virtual fear of the sinister Shamus Henry (whose heart I believe was the size of a pea). Mr. Gil was inclined to stay more than a few steps ahead at all times, regardless the costs. It would not be out of line to speculate that this was a source of amusement for Shamus Henry, as he liked to see people jump. And if you can make the big Texan jump, it is worth at least two points.

They say all great leaders inspire hatred. Shamus Henry was not a great leader, but he certainly did <u>inspire</u> something. Usually one season was enough for anyone, except for that foolish Texan who came back for seconds. Knucklehead. I might have complained that Mr. Gil was hard on us, but truly, he was hardest upon himself. Above all, Gil hated to be caught with his legendary pants down. Personally, living in close proximity to legend was challenging enough without such complications, which did nothing to sweeten ole Gil's disposition. Gil might have been inspired to say *it is lonely at the top*... but its good to remember that it is lonely at the bottom too — so how do you know which end you are at?

Allow me to flesh out the image a bit more. Firstly, Mr. Gil sported a large mustache to accent his Texas persona. You may think this unremarkable, but Gil insisted it was the best woman trap ever invented. Personally, I thought it likened him to a goofy walrus. Nonetheless, Mr. Gil felt that no worthwhile woman could resist his voluminous lip ornament. Yessir, they was like the proverbial moth to the flame.

"Oh Gil, can ah' touch it?" *"Why sure darlin,'"* he would purr.

Who knew if any of his stories could be believed — personally, I am content to rely upon gossip and besides, I did not see any of the other fellows hot on growing one. After dinner, Mr. Gil would commence to preen that fool mustache with his fork. Any comments about having particles of food stuck therein produced a matter of fact "of course I do," with just the right Texas twAang. On occasion, Gil would add to the ambiance by "letting one rip," proclaiming, *"Its just like my Grandma used to say... 'Sometimes there's more room on the outside than on the inside.'"* Definitely more than I needed to know.

The guests found this nearly as amusing as when he filed his toenails with a horseshoeing file, which fit neatly into Gil's well-orchestrated act of schmoozing tips. This stunt was saved for the best of prospects — so when Gil got out the big horseshoeing file you knew he was hot on the trail of Big Daddy and moving in for the kill. That look of pure bullshit would cross his eyes as he laid it on nice and thick. A snake in disguise — he would snatch off the 5-gallon Festus hat and clutch it to his heart, smiling like he was innocent or something. Made a person wish right then for hip boots, and I'd swear there was a faint sickly smell in the air. I referred to this act as Gil "romancing the bone." Gil definitely did not like that.

No tale too tall (nor mud waller too low) for the contradictory Gil was a man of great height and depth. Trick was to figure out from which end he was operating at any given time. It would not do for Mr. Gil to learn that he had gotten under your skin. Best to adopt a look of pure boredom, or ignore him altogether. The Texan hated to be ignored, so eventually he would leave you alone.

Gil once made point that I was *"one of the very few women in the North Buffalo Valley Wilderness— least wise young, single and* <u>*somewhat*</u> *attractive. He featured that if"n I was a sportin' woman, I could make myself a tidy bit of money."* (Picture that 'cat that et the mouse' smirk on his face.) Confessed that he *"didn't give a fig about all those other cowboys. They could fend for themselves. He was just trying to keep his OWN bedroll warm."* Delightful. I was getting all kind of pictures, none of which was very pretty. I caught a look at his naked behind once when he was taking a solar shower – and IT was not pretty.

"Mr. Gil, accordin' to some of them things I have heard about them cowboys, if **YOU** *was a sportin' man, you might make yourself* **a whole lot MO' money!"** His mustachioed face puffed up crimson red as he hissed, *"that ain't even* <u>FUNNY</u>*!"* With that Gil promptly huffed off, spurs a' clanging in the distance, and there was no more speculation about making extra money in the hills.

One morning I arose to the quiet splendor of the backcountry. Birds twittered in the cool morning air, Joy Creek running cold and clear nearby, light morning mist ghosting the tree line with the sun just peeking over the tops. This was surely a slice of paradise. Scanning the tranquil green pastures I breathed a sigh of wonder and gratitude – until my eyes came to rest upon

the spectacle of Mr. Gil taking his morning constitutional. I tell you, that Texan was always messing up the scenery, one way or another. Looked something like the cowboy version of the pink flamingo. It has occurred to me that the world might just be ready for a new era of tacky lawn ornaments?

One morning Mr. Gil headed out on the weekly run to town. This entailed a 30-mile horseback ride from Hawk's Rest to Turpin Meadows Trailhead, along with the *perfunctory* trip to the bar scene, followed by a quick turnaround back to Hawk's Rest the next morning – which was brutal. We expected Gil to show up anytime with some seriously needed supplies when the local rangers stopped by with a message. Gil had been in a wreck, overturned his truck driving back from town. Seems he had started falling asleep and snapped awake in time to find wildlife crossing the road — well that is what he claimed. Now he was in the hospital with a bruised low back and a broken nose. I hear tell that the nurses were under penalty of death not to touch the mustache, unless by some acceptable means of pleasure. The mustache remained undesecrated.

While this certainly put a lot of hardship on the rest of the crew, I will confess that life was a wee bit easier without the troublemaking Gil around to stir up conflict in the ranks. This allowed the other guys a chance to handle more responsibility and prove themselves, especially without ole' Gil hogging the spotlight. Me, I was just happy to be left to my peace. As amusing as Gil could be, he was not altogether nice, nor entirely sane, and definitely not a full 100-watt bulb. I went so far as to muse that I wished he would not come back. Which, when he did come back, I was confronted with directly. I said, *"Gil, if you weren't so busy being a jerk and generally dispensing misery, I would not feel that way, now would I?"* Gil did not like that, but for once he could not dispute it.

One night, late in the hunting season when I was suffering the most rigorous of schedules (getting up at 2:30 in the morning to start breakfast, returning to bed from 6:00 to 12:00, then working until 11:00 pm...) Gil had the poor taste to complain about my cooking. This, after I had kept it hot and waiting long after everyone had gone to bed. This, after Shamus Henry had cut back on my grocery list yet again, making it ever more difficult to manage. Shamus Henry had this theory that I could make food taste just as good with <u>half</u> the ingredients, which was without doubt a financially driven perspective. I replied, *"Gil, you have been saying all along how your Southern Baptist Grandma raised you strict to have good manners. To date, I have seen little of 'em! Right now you have a choice:*

> *Eat, and **shut up**… or DON'T eat, and **shut up**…*
> *either way I am certain you get the message."*

Gil sputtered a few threats about *making life difficult* for the remainder of the season. I asked how a *month of the trots* sounded, and suggested he quit while he still had enough in him to be a shithead.

Yes, gravity and resistance eventually catches up with the best of us, even Texans – and so toward the end of the season Mr. Gil met with another bit of misfortune while adjusting the pigging strings (ropes) on the pack string. Got his thumb in the way just as a packhorse pulled back, cinching the rope, and <u>off it popped</u>, just like a daisy. We had just passed him on the trail not an hour before, and when we got to camp to find the holocaust he had left behind, we were thinking none too kind of his well-being. I am not mean by nature, but you could not help but feel it was due payment for all the nasty things we had endured throughout the season. You see, Gil was not happy unless he was making someone else miserable, just playing with their heads all the time until you wanted to take his own set of spurs to his Texas behind.

Now Mr. Gil must go through life enduring bad hitchhiking jokes, and wondering if people secretly call him as NUB. Helluva thing to happen to a legend! I declare, had he left that legendary thumb in its usual hiding place, this might never have happened. Even so, Mr. ImPOSSible is certain to weave exciting tales, (and land himself some tail) around the mystery of the missing thumb. Perhaps a raging grizzly snapped it off, and like the unfortunate Captain Hook, pursues poor Gil to this day, wanting the rest of it? As Gil was particularly fond of saying, *shit happens in the woods.*

In my memory that was another hellish job for which I was ill fitted. Sure I got to see some beautiful wildernesses, but it nearly cost me a thing called sanity, and I have never wanted to be a man. After five months of feeling backed into a corner I had a mean temper and a short fuse. As such, it was the last of my days as an outfitter cook. I threw in my spatula (for awhile) and headed off to better things. In retrospect, I am inclined to name a special dinner after the fair and legendary Gil Hoss — Shithead Stew seems fitting, though he would not be pleased with that either.

As for the dreaded Shamus Henry, King of rationing candy bars (even to paying guests) and skimping on the crew's grocery list... when the guys used to gripe that there was not enough meat after a long day's work, he would sometimes brag how he could *"go out in that yonder field and GRaaAZE if he had to..."* One day I finally lost my temper and said "Go ahead, and strip naked too so you will blend in with the cows (you stingy bastard). Shamus Henry did not like that, nor my further suggestion that he let the boys through the food line before heaping his own plate. But then he did not like me anyway. Kind of comes with the territory when you are in the company of a few good assholes. I tend to think his comeuppance will come around as well, though I like to imagine it will not be his thumb that gets caught in the pigging string. One can hope.

COON PATE' *

I have decided that Coon Pate' really compliments an old Texas nuisance like Gil Hoss, and besides, I have been itching to use this somewhere....

½ - ¾ lb	liver (any kind will do) hot from boiling in water.
1-6 oz. Pkg.	Philadelphia Cream Cheese (or more)
4	green onions (leaves and all)
1 T.	olive oil
¼ tsp.	nutmeg
1 tsp.	garlic, minced (more if you like more garlic)
¼ C.	Sherry
½ tsp.	salt (or less to taste)
½ tsp.	pepper (or less to taste)
	Dash of Tabasco (hot sauce)

Put all ingredients into the blender. Use the cream cheese and the Sherry to control the consistency. It will harden some once in the fridge but get it nice and thick in the blender. Then put in a container and place in the fridge to cool. Enjoy

*Nutria or raccoon liver is rumored to make a delicious pate. Recipe courtesy of Clarence D. Snyder better known as "Doc", and borrowed with permission from Dennis Fisher's Wild Game Recipes at www.fishersnet.com. Copyright © 1995, 1996, 1997, 1998 Dennis Fisher.

WULFIE THE WONDER MULE

I wish I had written things down way back when it was all happening. Seems I have forgotten so much, but I do recall some funny moments here and there. Especially one quirky mule that I believe warrants its own paragraph in history. Just utter its name, and any of the fellows will set to sputtering story after story — all ending in frustration, or maybe laughter now that so much time has passed. Time does indeed make the misery seem milder. Introducing Wulfie the Wonder Mule.

It is doubtful that his origins are noted in any prestigious registry of mule history, yet without doubt, Wulfie has left his mark on any number of impressionable young wranglers, be it their egos or their behinds. Wulfie is what we call an "orangutan" — *something that conducts itself without reason, and without warning*. I am somewhat shy to confess that I did at some point begin to understand his intentions, which I would never have admitted at the time. *To think like a mule is to be compared to one.* I prefer to spare myself that comparison.

Firstly, like most any mule, Wulfie did what Wulfie wanted to do — and very little else. Just try and lead him down to the game hanging tree and pack a few elk quarters on him and you will soon know what I mean. Though I felt sorry for the wrangler charged with this duty, the spectacle of it was of such exceptional entertainment that I rarely missed the opportunity to observe – from a safe distance. How they ever got him packed is a matter of luck and persistence. Perhaps the Mule Deity was smiling down upon their sorry souls, or perhaps Wulfie was just funnin' with them. Nonetheless, packing game on Wulfie was nearly akin to giving birth – for which the greater percent of mankind is duly unprepared.

Another favorite game of Wulfie's I call "Flip the Packhorse." There was a certain pack bridge, spanning maybe 30 feet, on the North Fork Buffalo Valley trail. Of all the pack bridges on this trail, Wulfie never offered to cause trouble on any but this particular one. And OH did he cause trouble. The boys were accustomed to placing Wulfie on the tail end of the pack string, where Wulfie was content to let his contemporaries pull him along for the ride. But come to this bridge he would wait until the entire string was positioned on it (leaving only himself on land) then plant his feet firm. As the bridge had a noticeable angle where it met solid ground, Wulfie's antic had the disastrous effect of pulling the horses directly preceding him off balance, thereby sending them *ass over teakettle* into the deep ditch below, and usually upon their backs.

There is nothing so frightening to a wrangler as the sight of Shamus Henry's prized packed animal on its back, 10 feet below a narrow bridge with a bunch of pack animals above. Immediately all hands bale off, pack ropes cut (a major infraction in of itself) to free the unfortunate animal before it suffocates. This, followed by a good hour of reassembling one's shit before any further progress is made down the trail, if you're LUCKY. Wulfie just stands there looking innocent, and Wulfie is no fool for he never tries this when Shamus Henry is in company. But soon as Shamus Henry leaves the boys in charge (which was often), you could bet money he would be turning the world upside down again.

Of course, mules are not the only things known to be stubborn in the hills. There is a certain Texan whose logic about parallels a mule, and he was just as likely to plant his own feet firmly in the ground — so to speak. One day we were riding the trail with full pack strings and a bunch of guests. As we approached this bridge, I knew with complete certainty that Wulfie would pull his usual stunt. Meanwhile, the World Famous Texan had assigned me to bringing up the rear (alternately known as "picking up the pieces"), which put me eight horses behind Wulfie. I suggested that if I were to ride right up on Wulfie's tail, I might succeed in moving him across the bridge? Naturally Mr. Gil would not hear of it, and told me to "*just stay back there like he tole' me to do.*" If ever I had a mind to disobey, it would have been at that moment. But I didn't, and true to form, Wulfie did his thing dislodging not one but two horses off the bridge this time. One minute we were riding peaceably through this magnificent wilderness, next thing all hell breaks loose, everyone shouting, horses scattered through the trees and guests milling about confused — it was a pitiful sight. Alas, there was nothing I could do, 'cept to say, "I told ya so," which I did. And look upon the whole scene with disgust, which I did.

If ever it happened again that year, nobody admitted it and Shamus Henry was none the wiser. But if I were to keep score, I would say the half-breed jackass was at least three points ahead of the dimwitted Texan, and looking smarter all the time. Besides which, as neatly as Shamus Henry could ride that Texan, I am quite certain that no one ever rode Wulfie.

MULE BISCUITS*

In honor of Wulfie, here are some biscuits with a kick —

2 C.	flour
¾ tsp.	soda
½ tsp.	salt
¼ C.	shortening
¼ C.	vinegar
½ C.	milk

Cut shortening into dry ingredients, add milk/vinegar, and mix until just moistened. Pat dough about ½ inch thick onto a floured surface, cut and bake at 450°F degrees for 12 min.

* Another old family favorite from my mother, who has been known to possess a little piss and vinegar herself.

THE STAR WRANGLER

THE STAR WRANGLER

In every outfit, one wrangler above all others must shine, and Shamus Henry's camp was no exception. Meet Kevin, the Star Wrangler.

Kevin may have had a few things to learn about horse handling that first year, but as an established outdoorsman and hunter since childhood, he was an instant asset to the company. Young, strong and hardworking, Kevin soon gave the seasoned Gil a run for his Texas dollar. Gil was not fond of being upstaged, thus Kevin was in for a Stetson-full of abuse from that time on. (Do you see the pattern?)

Being a natural golden boy, Kevin won that special bit of attention and approval from Shamus Henry, which drove Gil plum wild. The more Gil hungered for approval, the more certain it was he would never get it. Worse yet, Shamus Henry seemed to derive a certain pleasure out of this game like it was the finest kind of entertainment. It goes without saying that Shamus Henry was a *five-letter prince* — which only served to up the ante. Gil would be pissing and moaning and generally causing discourse, where Kevin would just smile and head off to chop wood or whatever chore was at hand. I believe he enjoyed the workout and the challenge. Gil, albeit a hard worker, seemed more in love with the status of being a foreman, and the illusion of being an almost legend. Kevin soon became accustomed to receiving "the death look."

Gil's favorite pastime was to loll about after dinner and brag on his conquests during days off in town. Gil knew full well Kevin had poor luck with the ladies, and he played that sore spot to the hilt. One night, Gil sat preening that long foolish mustache, reminiscing about the latest lady to pass its way. With that familiar *cat that 'et the mouse* look, he purred, *"Hey Keeevin, ya wont ta smell my mustache?"* Without hesitation, Kevin snorted, *"No thanks, I already know what **DICK** smells like."* Gil should have realized he was out-brained right then — naturally he did not.

One might wish that Gil would remember that old saying about getting more bees with honey than vinegar — but he didn't, so the war went on. There is nothing as entertaining as a couple of men trying to best each other, especially when one has the advantage of seniority (which he may draw upon when all else fails) and the other quite simply shines. Which one suffered the hardest? Who can say, but I know who paid in the end.

Kevin did get his chance to sparkle when Gil was kind enough to roll his truck and incapacitate himself for a month or so. Long enough for Kevin to step into the spotlight and put himself to the test (as did the other guys). They all did an excellent job. It was inevitable that Gil would return, and return he did — with a vengeance. From that day on, Kevin (along with yours truly) was a 'suffering all over again.

At one point, the friction became fierce as Gil stepped up his daily doses of antagonism and Kevin was near breaking point. Finally I asked Gil to back off so we could have some peace in camp – that danged fool was playing with fire. Gil ought to have recalled in his little pea brain that Kevin held a black belt in karate— but his Texas machismo overrode such details and presumably a good old-fashioned cowboy sucker punch would take care of business proper. Without doubt Kevin could have kicked both the hot air AND the stuffing out of him. While Gil certainly deserved this, I preferred not to pick up the sorry pieces, assuming there'd be ANY pieces lying about when Kevin was through with him. Under different circumstances, I would have paid money to watch, but here everyone's job was tough enough without casualties lying around, and besides, their ill humor was becoming evident to the guests.

I suppose Gil was getting his last licks in before hunting season. Little did he realize, (or perhaps he did?) that once the hunt began he would never be able to touch Kevin again. Worse yet, he would pay in spades for the many months of abuse visited upon Kevin — every trespass and every boast would come back to haunt him for Kevin was by far a superior hunter and guide.

When hunting season did come around, Gil was sweating bullets, though he did his best to hide it. He had been shooting off his mouth the entire year prior about how he would like a shot at being a full-fledged guide. Now Gil was in the hot seat as those same hunters had returned, fully expectant to see a fine display of sportsmanship. As the old saying goes, you can bullshit all you like, but after the first five minutes you had better possess something to back it up. Gil was being upstaged again by the golden boy (which didn't take much) and it was a sorry sight.

Quite naturally, Kevin was doing what he had practices all his life and having a blast. Kevin's hunters were thrilled as they had paid a lot of money to hunt elk, and not only was Kevin an excellent guide, he was FUN. Kevin's hunters shared the day's tales at the nightly dinner table with laughter and joy, as Gil's hunters looked like a couple of Pissed-Off-Petes trying hard to hold back a few choice words. Gil glowered in the corner for he was contemplating murder. I wonder but he might have had some voodoo effigy of Kevin squirreled away in his tent. But no matter, not a hair on that golden head ever got damaged, and the hunting season came to its usual conclusion.

Fortunately for Mr. Gil, the Star Wrangler did pull a couple of boners now and then.

One day Shamus Henry was conferring with a group of hunters as the crew readied to pack them out with their game. Shamus Henry had just sent his golden boy off with a mule for that purpose, along with a pointed reminder that he had **best** not lead that mule off without lashing down those wooden panniers. But Kevin was prone, on occasion, to cut corners, and at that same moment the loose panniers clanked causing the mule to shy, causing the panniers to clang and bang even louder. The entire group was then treated to the spectacle of that mule bucking every last remnant of equipment off its back, bashing it in the process. The Star Wrangler was red-faced and helpless in its wake. About the funniest wrangler moment of the season and I allowed myself the indiscretion of laughing aloud.

Shamus Henry was disgusted. Gil was heartily pleased.

PRIME RIB*

What with all the humor and nonsense, what could be more appropriate than a good old fashioned Prime RIB?

1	prime rib cut

1 C.	Worcestershire Sauce
1 C.	Cabernet Wine
1 tsp.	granulated onion
1 tsp.	granulated garlic
½ tsp.	white pepper

Trim meat, punch holes with fork and pour sauce over meat in pan (use no-stick spray). Coat meat with more granulated onion and garlic. Bake at 350°F for 2-3 hours (depending upon size of roast) uncovered. Baste with sauce, rehydrate as needed.

Check meat temperature and remove at 130-135°F. Let rest under lights for 30 minutes. Roast will continue cooking to 140°F

Serve with side of *au jus* if desired.

* Recipe courtesy of a previous cook at Coulter Lake Guest Ranch.

GOLDEN DINNER ROLLS*

2 pkgs.	active dry yeast
2 C.	warm water
½ C.	sugar
2 tsp.	salt
¼ C.	vegetable oil
1	egg
7 C.	flour

In a large glass bowl, dissolve warm water, yeast and sugar (do not use metal utensils). Set this bowl inside a larger bowl or pan containing warm water and allow a few minutes to activate yeast.

Mix in salt, oil and egg. Add flour several cups at a time and mix well (may use electric mixer). Do not knead. Place dough in a greased bowl and cover with waxed paper and a damp cloth. Dough may be kept in refrigerator for several days until ready to use, or left at room temperature to rise for immediate use. For lighter rolls, do not knead – dough will be somewhat sticky. For a heavier consistency (hamburger rolls), knead lightly on a floured surface.

Once dough has risen, roll out (1 / 2" thick) on a floured surface using greased rolling pin. Use greased round cutter for dinner rolls, fold each circle in half and brush with butter before setting on pan to rise. For hamburger rolls, cut larger squares. Cover and let rise in warm place until desired. Bake at 400°F until golden brown, approx. 12-15 minutes. Brush with melted butter and serve.

*These light dinner rolls are a long-time favorite on the dinner table at Coulter Lake Guest Ranch.

DIAMOND DAVE

schucks

DIAMOND DAVE

I call him Diamond Dave because he was something of a gem in the rough – mostly rough. Also,
because he had previously worked at some
guest ranch that called itself Diamond Some-
thing-Or-Other. Besides, Dave was testament that even bullshit can sparkle
and you could hardly miss him unless he happened to be standing sideways. Just picture one tall skinny blue-eyed blond kid who would have you
believe he was the real kind of cowboy, unless you happen to find out he
sprang from Phoenix, Arizona. Dave was a cocky piece of work who was
relieved of his former job at the Diamond outfit due to his refusal to rake
rocks. Real men do not rake rocks. Thus Dave came to us by default, through
no real fault of his own except a good dose of ole-fashioned pigheadedness.
Naturally, he was in good company.

Dave was a hard working young man and on this count, no one could dis-
count him. I suspect Dave came from somewhat humble beginnings, so naturally, championed the underdog and since there was no lower dog than Mr.
Gil, they soon became fast friends and cohorts in misery – sticking together
through thick and thin. Shamus Henry liked to pit us against each other, and
Dave was an especially valuable ally – Mr. Gil set the pace and Dave followed
like a faithful dog.

And what a fierce dog he was – Dave liked everyone to know that he wasn't afraid of nothin' in the world. Indeed, he was a tough scrap – the kind of guy that might not be the most refined fighter, but I suspect he could take punch and keep coming back for more as if he felt no pain. Dave would listen to all the stories about grizzly bear encounters (never having encountered one himself) and boast, *"I ain't scared of no bear. Don't scare me a BIT!"* My God he was a piece of work. If Dave ever was scared, he did not admit it. Not until one fateful night during hunt season when there was no hope of pretension.

The Star Wrangler and his hunter returned well after dark with their prize elk quartered and strapped to the saddle. Dave, being one of two camp jacks, had the dubious honor of having to hang the meat and take care of the horses. You have to picture the setting to really appreciate it. Night after night, these guys were duly reminded that they were never alone when they encountered fresh grizzly tracks over their own recent tracks on the way back to camp in the darkness. This could be somewhat unsettling. So when Dave and Harry struck off down that snowy dark trail to the bear pole (which was well away from camp, and where the bears had already stolen a couple of elk quarters for a snack) you could imagine what it might feel like to be walking in their boots.

Back at camp, Mr. Gil is busy bullshitting and trying to maintain his declining status, since yet another elk had been bagged through no thanks to him. The happy hunter is retelling his adventure to the other fellas who offered congratulations. Over the excitement I heard cries for help wafting up from the river. All ears cocked until we could discern more clearly, *"It's a BEAR, it's a BEEEEAR ... HELLLLP!!! I'm gonna DIE!!! WILL, bring the gun!"Gil SAVE me!*

All season long Gil had been waiting for his moment to reclaim his command — and here it was. Gil set his mustache to full throttle and it was full reveille in Camp Hell with all hands grabbing pistolas and heading off to the river. Boss retrieved his revolver from the packsaddle and commenced to shooting off rounds, right by my ear. I was holding the only lantern, so my first thought was to run down with everyone else and lend some light. But I stopped short – for without doubt the macho men would tell me to stay in camp. (By now, I was used to this.) Shamus Henry growled *"You git on down there"* until he realized who was holding the lantern, then indeed ordered me to keep camp. Meanwhile the fracas continued with guns going off and men yelling in the darkness. I prayed no one was being carved up at the bear pole, and felt somewhat relieved that I was spared the pleasure of joining them. I made no claims of having no fear of bears.

With the dawning of next morning's sun, the full story came to light. Dave and Harry had set to the task of hanging the four elk quarters. Dave was high up on the game rigging, which amounted to four thick logs lashed horizontally between two huge trees, and a pulley to haul the meat up and hang it on hooks. Harry had been banging around the hills for years and hunted his share of game — very little fazed him. Dave however was finally hitting his limit. Even 20 feet up on that bear pole was not high enough to ease his nerves. Harry was alone on the ground with all that elk meat, puffing the usual cigarette and doing his job when Dave caught sight of two yellow eyes glowering at the edge of the flashlight beam. I suppose it is somewhat understandable that he would come unglued.

Dave chattered there was *some eyes* looking at him, and he was sure it was a bear. Harry poopawed him and said, *"that ain't no bear,"* and continued working. Dave countered that it WAS a bear, and if Harry did not haul his ass up the ladder to safety, Dave was going to kick off the ladder forthwith, and leave Harry to fend for himself. Dave then commenced to squealing like a girl and there was nothing in the world that could have shut him up.

The next morning the men did a thorough job of checking for tracks in the snow, and they surmised it was most likely a fisher or pine martin that had been attracted by the smell of the elk meat. No bear tracks, not even a respectable bear turd. Dave was up for the roasting of his life and the men were all too happy to comply. *"Say DAVE, seen any BEARS lately?"* Dave would buck up and retort, ***"Straight onta hell, all of ya!"*** The cook tent shook with laughter. Dave took it all in stride and after a time nobody rubbed any more salt in the remnants of Dave's wounded ego. But you can be sure; we never again heard old Diamond Dave utter a single word about bears not scaring him a bit. Nothing at all.

Generally, Dave was a good sport with a light sense of humor, which was excellent for breaking tension around camp. The harder they sweated, the harder they worked up the humor. Dave was fond of guttural Mexican cuss words, which became a favorite pastime, along with his best British limey accent. On one of the more amusing days, Dave and Kevin were busy cutting lodge poles for the cook tent when the two of them veered off into a game of Samurai cowboy. An impromptu sparring match with the 20 foot poles, right there in the open field, complete with mock Japanese howling. What are the chances that some wrangler from another camp would happen to ride out of the trees at just that moment? Yup, a million to one. But he did and I still laugh every time I think of it.

And fortunately, Dave was a gentle hand with the horses and mules, for those horses bore staggering burdens from June through October, each hauling 160 or more pounds of pack upon their backs through heat, horseflies and snow — regardless. Not to mention overweight hunters from dawn till dusk at high elevations. A little kindness goes a long way for such horses and mules. And Dave had a heart of gold. He spent most of the season working on a particular little shadow paint named Smokey, transforming him from a lazy untried horse to a steady disciplined mount. And because Dave was usually level headed, few of the horses' antics rattled him. These are good traits in a wrangler. I often got the feeling that despite the backbreaking work, Dave just enjoyed being alive, and being a man in the company of good men. Dave did not take so well to me, because I did not enjoy backbreaking work. I tended to want to keep my back in one piece, and I detested packing up camp every two weeks just so's I could set it up some 30 miles away for another two weeks. I have never managed to do a very good job of anything that I detested, and therefore won myself a bit of hostility from the guys. Fortunately, I was a decent cook.

In all fairness, all the guys were hard workers, and though their jobs might have seemed glamorous to an outsider or impressionable young boy, in truth, it was a kind of hell. Not the kind of profession a guy wants to maintain till the golden years because this job would make him old well before that time. Every year there were fallen trees blocking endless miles of wilderness trails – all which had to be chopped and moved by somebody. Gil, Kevin and Dave were this year's "some bodies," and they whacked a whole lot of woody. When there wasn't wood to chop, there were horses to wrangle. Any given day there was a new form of hell to challenge the guys – horses running off; horses kicking off their hobbles for which Shamus Henry would place bounties upon the guys heads if they failed to locate them; camp to be set up; latrines to be dug in hard rocky soil; water to haul, camp to be torn down. Then came hunt season and late night horse wrangling, followed by 4:00 am horse wrangling wherein cold hands struggled to remove frozen snowy hobbles off from the horses' legs in the dark. Now that was my idea of purgatory. Never was there a shortage of work in camp. If a guy made it through a full season he was then awarded the right to claim membership to the Survivor's Club – where he could tell stories, even make them up if he wanted to for the rest of his life. I have taken further liberty to WRITE the stories – hopefully the guys won't mind.

Wherever Diamond Dave may be as I write this, you can be almost certain that he is working hard, smoking hard, and brightening those around him with his natural good-humored ways. We certainly suffered some trials together, and I have since forgiven him for promising to run me down if he ever laid eyes on me again.

QUICK CHICKEN SOUTHWEST

You might agree, a "quick" chicken (from the Southwest no less) seems appropriate here.

4 pc.	chicken breasts (boneless optional)

MARINADE

¼ C.	lime juice
¼ C.	vegetable or olive oil
2 T.	parsley or cilantro, chopped
1 tsp.	garlic, chopped

TOPPING

8 slices	Cheddar or Monterey Jack cheese
1 C.	thick salsa, heated
	avocado slices

Combine marinade ingredients in a plastic bag. Add chicken and marinate for four hours in refrigerator. Bake chicken at 325°F for approximately 40 minutes; add salsa and cheese for remaining five minutes. Serve on rice.

THE FLORIDA SUITE

Summer was drawing to a close, and the crew had begun the arduous task of setting up hunt camp. This entailed packing out all the lightweight summer equipment and raising thick, heavy canvas tents on wooden frames in its place. Collapsible wood stoves would then be packed in, and endless stacks of wood must be chopped to feed them. Shamus Henry announced that some 9-10 cords would have to be cut and stacked, which, when you're standing in a designated wilderness area, is a formidable task since no chain saws are allowed. Huge Lodge Pole pine, often several feet thick (and already dead) would be felled and sectioned by hand, hauled in by horse, cut with a two-man saw and then split. You know the old saying about firewood warming a man twice... well in this case, I believe it was more like five times.

With such a mountain of work at hand, I am certain the guys were somewhat dying inside (I would have been), but this was one of those times when the term "cowboy up" got a lot of use. Needless to say, firewood was a golden commodity and not to be wasted.

In the midst of all this preparation, the last of our summer guests arrived — two women gynecologists from Florida. Naturally they found our nighttime climate just a tad cold and it was not long before the firewood was being put to use. Every chunk of wood that went into that stove pained the boys like it was their first born, but they cowboyed up and kept quiet for the most part. Their one indiscretion was to dub the girls' tent "the Florida Suite" since they maintained it like a virtual sauna. Had the girls asked, I am sure the boys would have suggested less wasteful ways of keeping warm... but they never did ask.

As the girls enjoyed leisurely trail rides and explorations, the guys set to the chore of hauling and cutting wood. Mr. Gil was in full glory because his stout horse "Tinkerbell" was the only horse in camp dependable for dragging logs. This reaffirmed Gil's dominant status over the rest of the guys, in his own mind and Gil was only too pleased to put on a show for the girls, with spurs, chaps and Festus hat, talkin' real intimate to ole' Tink and inspiring him to do virtual wonders. Just a man and his horse — kind of like the cowboy equivalent to the phallic sports car. Gil hunkered down in the saddle and I swear he was nearly blinded by the sheer magnitude of himself.

WORLD FAMOUS GILL ON SUPER TINK

The girls and I stood back kind of laughing to ourselves. Finally I had to have a little fun at Gil's expense, so I says, *"Hey Gil, the girls here think you look mighty impressive up in that there saddle, only they think you ought to scooch up in the stirrups just a bit..."* (Get it? Gynecologists? Stirrups?) Gil said he didn't know what that meant, but he did not like it. Cookie gets the death look.

One evening the boys made a few jokes about "the Florida Suite," to which Kevin added, *"Now all we needed was a few pink flamingoes and some Cubans and it'd be just like Florida."* The brunette girl's face dropped in shock — she was Cuban. Way to go Kev — you sure know how to make a favorable impression! Yes, even his status as Star Wrangler could not save him now. I quietly left the table. Ignorance, like water, finds it own level, and this was one of those times I was embarrassed by it.

Now during all this time there was a bit of intrigue going on. The guys were nearly convinced that the two ladies were — well, they were a couple. And suspecting this, the guys were on the lookout for evidence to either support or disprove that theory. They strutted their stuff and spied all at once, hoping for a small glimmer of attraction, or a forbidden caress to explain why they were not receiving due attention. It was the topic of much private discussion. Gil made the only assumption a man like him could come up with — which was that the younger one had been seduced by the older one, and all she needed was a man like him to straighten her around. Oh ya, that'd fix her up proper Gil. I'm sure every female yearns for the touch of a legend like your-self, if only for the knowledge that she'll be referred to as a whore during your fireside chats for years to come.

The boys never did figure the answer to that equation, and probably never realized how obvious their foolishness was to the girls. But diverse cultures come together, even in the backcountry of Wyoming and sometimes we learn from one another. But when we part we are all still who we are and who we have a right to be. With that, we go back to our homes where the most com-pelling images become our memories.

I imagine whenever those ladies recall their trip to Wyoming, certain things come to mind, and what I wouldn't give to be a fly on the wall for those conversations. Perhaps in time the pure idiocy of the boys will have dimin-ished, and maybe it is the cool mountain air, the wide expansive beauty, and the smell of wood in the fire that will linger? I extend a fair bit of credit for their having come out to the backcountry at all. Wyoming is a far haul from Florida, and to say that it is a different world is an understatement. There are no familiar pink flamingoes or palm trees, and as Kevin the Star Wrangler discovered, only a rare Cuban now and then —

I consider it a cultural obligation, as well as a necessary part of their wrangler enlightenment program, to include a taste of Cuban culture herein — just on the outside chance that one of the boys might see it, and be saved from complete and utter ignorance.

PARRILLADA DE POLLO "FLORIDA" AL JUGO CITRICO*
(Citrus-Grilled Florida Chicken)

4-6	boneless, skinless chicken breasts or thighs
1 C.	orange juice
¼ C.	fresh lime juice
2 T.	extra-virgin olive oil
1/3 C.	fresh cilantro, washed & finely chopped (set aside whole sprigs for garnish)
3	garlic cloves, minced
2 tsp.	ground cumin
	salt to taste
½ tsp.	crushed red pepper flakes
	orange sections and lime wedges for garnish

Place chicken breasts in a large shallow baking dish. In a medium bowl, whisk together the orange and lime juices, oil, cilantro, garlic, cumin, 1 teaspoon salt and the red pepper flakes. Pour the marinade over chicken, turning to coat well. Cover and marinate at least eight hours or overnight, turning the breasts once or twice.

Preheat the grill to medium. Pour the marinade into a saucepan, bring to a rolling boil for one full minute. Oil the grill. Place the breasts, on the grill and brush generously with the marinade. Cover and grill, basting several times, for about 8 minutes, or until the chicken is done. Turn the chicken over and grill, basting, for about 8 minutes longer, or until browned and cooked through.

Transfer chicken to a platter. Garnish with cilantro sprigs, orange sections, lime wedges, and serve.

* Recipe courtesy of Raúl Musibay of the Three Guys From Miami's excellent website featuring Cuban cuisine and culture. http://icuban.com. Enjoy!

CUBAN BLACK BEAN SOUP

2 C.	black beans
5 cloves	garlic
1 T.	salt
1½ tsp.	cumin
1½ tsp.	oregano
2 med.	onions
2	hot green chilies
3 T.	olive oil
1 T.	water

Soak beans (covered) in cold water overnight. Drain, cook in 2 quarts of water, covered, until tender.

Crush together garlic, salt, cumin and oregano. Chop onions and chilies, place in skillet, add garlic/spice mixture and cook in oil until onions are clear. Stir in tablespoon of water and cook until tender. Add mixture to soup and simmer to meld flavors.

LONESOME DOVE'S BEST KEPT SECRET

Lonesome Dove was a medium-sized gray roan mare of no particular visual significance. She may have earned the name Lonesome because she was not wont for the company of her contemporaries, nor did the guys want anything to do with her. Dove's walk was more like a trot and after 30 miles of her pulling hard at the mouth to go faster, not one of the guys would lead the string off her — which is why I was often designated to ride Dove during the summer of Shamus Henry's employ. I suppose they thought they were slighting me somehow, but I never minded. Dove was strong and dependable and she was not known for dragging behind like some of those fat ole male Quarter horses. Dove could kick their butts most any day. It was not until the hunt season months later that I learned something of her past.

The first year in the backcountry is the toughest on any unseasoned horse and it is known to take about three years to make a good mountain horse out of the average equine. Taken from a life of easy and predictable feed, the newcomer must learn which alpine grasses maintain bodyweight and how best to preserve their precious energy. It is not unusual for a first year horse to lose so much weight as to become nearly skeletal by season's end. By the third year, that horse has either gotten religion or perished.

Dove's first year was no different, and it was not long before she was an emaciated shadow of her once proud self. A long-time hunting guide told how a rather compassionless wrangler had ridden her to the ground until she finally collapsed, which is a rather critical indication for a horse. That fool wrangler stayed on and literally raked her sides bloody with his spurs. One wonders if he might have gouged her straight to the bone if the guide had not finally pulled him off and given him the business. I suspect that wrangler ruined her in a way — broke her spirit for good. Dove was never more than a vacant workhorse after that — as if nobody was home when you looked into her eyes. Dove may have shunned all affection or doting, but one thing was certain – she always did her job.

One day, when I was finally at my whit's end with my job and following a bit of hard truth from Gil, I insisted that he pack me out to the trailhead. Things had turned sour in camp, with me on one side of it, and the guys on the other. Either some issues were going to be cleared up or I was quitting the outfit. This was no small decision when you understand that I rarely release myself from my own promises – and I had <u>promised</u> to stay the whole season through. *(Yes, the chains that bind us best are the ones we choose ourselves.)* Still I could not imagine two more months of this kind of hell and I finally had to concede defeat.

Gil grudgingly saddled up Dove, Tinkerbell and one pack mule, and we headed out. For a time, I followed behind (as was customary) staring at the back of his fool head. Finally I thought better of it and trotted past. Gil did not protest, and I would not have cared if he had. From then on it was just Dove and me, and she was in a mind to cover some miles. For the first time in months I was alone and I felt free. I no longer cared if the job worked out or if I ever saw those messengers from purgatory again. I had been backed into a corner too long and I did not like the person I had become. In truth, I barely recognized myself anymore.

A short time later, I was visited by a momentary vision of myself being unseated and of Dove trotting away. I somewhat discounted the thought, but also took it as a wise reminder to pay attention and at all cost keep hold of the reins. I should have paid more attention.

A mile or so down the trail, some creature made the bushes quiver at 11:00 o'clock, Dove's ears pricked, and she subsequently sidestepped to about 3:00 o'clock, leaving me spinning at midnight. Essentially, I was airborne, somer-

saulting in mid-flight like the Charlie Brown
cartoon. Rather than cussing or squawking,
the only words to escape were a disgruntled
"*Awwwwww Dove.*" I hit the ground hard,
complete with dust cloud, the likes of which
only Pigpen could be envious. I do not recall seeing any point-studded logs in that
comic strip, but I landed alarmingly close
to one in my own private skit, ripping my
pants on one of the stubs and earning myself a nasty bruise that took months to disappear. I looked up just as Dove's hoof was
about to land in my chest, but she caught
herself and stepped back just in time. Natu-

THE PIVOTAL MOMENT...

rally, the wind got knocked out of me, but miraculously, Dove had not run
down the trail. Even with that full 360-degree aerial display (something I
never want to repeat) those reins remained firm in my grip and Dove was
still on the other end of them. Nostrils flaring, she pulled back tentatively.
Seemed she half expected me to beat her, but God I never appreciated her
more. I collected my bruised behind, hopped on and kept riding towards the
trailhead.

The only incriminating evidence, being the torn pants, were disposed of and
no one was the wiser – 'cept Dove and she doesn't tell secrets anyways.

DOVE DUMPLINGS *

I have never partaken of this "Dove Dumplings," recipe, but I know something of what it feels like to be one!

10-12	dove or quail breasts
¼ C.	vegetable oil
	Salt, pepper and onion to taste
2 C.	flour
1 tsp.	salt
¼ C.	shortening
2	eggs, beaten
¼ C.	milk
	2 cubes chicken bullion

Rinse dove well; pat dry. Brown in skillet with oil; drain. Place the dove in a stockpot and barely cover with water. Add salt, pepper, and onion. Simmer, covered, until meat is tender

Combine flour and salt in a mixing bowl. Add in shortening, mixing until crumbly. Stir in eggs and enough milk to form soft dough. Roll the dough out on a floured surface to about 1/8" thickness. Cut into 2-inch squares.

Remove dove from stockpot. Add chicken boullion to the stock and bring to a boil. Drop in dumplings one at a time. Cook for about 20 minutes or until tender. Return dove to stockpot and simmer covered for about 5 minutes.

*This was one of Dennis Fisher's favorites from when he was a kid. You can use just about any kind of wild bird for this recipe, he likes it best with dove or quail. Find this and a treasuretrove of other recipes at www.fishersnet.com.

SNICKERDOODLES*

Light fluffy cookies that my Mama used to make… my dear friend Whitney once likened them to *"little mattresses with sugar on top."* Wish I'd had a few to soften the landing from Dove's impromptu dumping.

4 X		6 X
2 C.	shortening	3 C.
6 C.	sugar	9 C.
8	eggs	12
4 T.	vanilla extract	6 T.
10 2/3 C.	flour	17 C.
8 T.	cream of tartar	10 T.
4 T.	baking soda	6 T.
1 T.	salt	1 ½ T.

Blend shortening, sugar, eggs & vanilla till smooth. In a separate bowl, blend dry ingredients thoroughly, add 1 cup at a time to wet mixture.

Make dollops on a lightly oiled cookie sheet. Sprinkle lightly with cinnamon and sugar and bake at 375°F for 8-12 minutes

*Another favorite recipe from Ma.

COWBOY WANNABE'S

Long time ago, when a man wore chaps, and spurs and other leather apparel, he depended upon them for his livelihood. Most likely he hand-crafted them personally, and you could bet he earned every rough and tough looking scar upon them. Nowadays, when a man dons leather accessories, the picture ain't quite that clear.

The West is filled with men who work the land and the livestock for a living. And likewise, it is filled with men who want to *look* like men who work the land and the livestock for a living. The latter fall under the heading of "wannabe's," and Lord, don't they <u>want</u> <u>to</u> <u>be</u>. (Still other types employ this garb for, shall we say, "horseplay," but we will not go there.)

I have seen all kinds of them in Jackson, Wyoming. Just hatched from some urban jungle, they will make a B-line for the local Corral West to load up on all the *perfunctory* cowboy attire. First, there is the striped Wrangler shirts, tight Wrangler jeans, a fancy pair of Hawthorn boots, and a nice new cowboy hat (stomp on it a few times so's you can tell how the bull threw ya).

Then comes the regulation oilskin duster. This piece of apparel was not intended for walking, but it sure looks sharp while you are struttin' your stuff down the street and besides, the tourists do not know any better. Yes, a formidable figure, a virtual cowboy superman with his cape — but wait? What's missing? LEATHER! Quick, down the street to the nearest leather shop. Man you got to get those chaps, or at least the shorter version popularly known as chinks. Either one will keep a cowboy dry and protected in the saddle. Chaps are leather leggings, which are essential to life on the range.

Besides, they look manly. Now add a leather vest, a pair of leather gloves, and top it off with a leather bolo for Sunday preaching (or Saturday night whorin') and you are just about set. What you need now is a good rugged set of spurs. Yes, this is critical gear if you are going to be a cowboy. If for nothing else than to add to the illusion that you might just use 'em on someone! Women will swoon at the mere thought of it.

WeeHa! Now you are nearly 100% set for the part. And here comes the final touch — on the way by the local drug store or gas station, mosey your *bad self* on up to the counter and order a case of Copenhagen. And say it like you mean it! Even if you know for a fact that chew has been reputed to cause mouth rot or that some brands of contain glass fiber to cut your gums so you get a stronger buzz. Even though you can count on it ruining your favorite beer, or fouling up the mechanics of a good spontaneous smooch, given you should be lucky enough to have a shot at one. And so what if you look like an old horse with a wad of it stuffed in your bottom lip. We are talking tradition here — TRADITION! (Naturally, I am writing this from the viewpoint of a woman.) And remember, do not spit into the wind.

Now there are a few things you will want to be picking up fast. Namely, the lingo. *Numero uno* is a saying that goes like this:

"Cowboy up."

Yes, you read it right. Simple as it may seem, this term says everything you need to know about being a wrangler/cowboy wannabe.

~   *Cowboy up* means, buck up, straighten up, put up AND shut up, do not whine or snivel until later when there ain't any women around.

~   *Cowboy up* means that if you get saddle sores — it will make you tougher, and by God you will never admit it!

~   *Cowboy up* means that if you have got to do something unpleasant, like rolling in sheep dip — it will make you tougher yet, and you will still like it.

~ *Cowboy up* means that if you're a'suffering from the worst camp cook of all time, you will eat gratefully, and like it.

~ *Cowboy up* means that even if you're a'feared for your life, you will snort in the face of danger, and like it. (Remember Dave & The Killer Bear!)

About the only thing a cowboy does get to complain about is when he runs out of chew or there is a shortage of women. Even if he is silently giving thanks to the Lord God Almighty, a shortage of chew is acceptable cause to complain. This is where some good old-fashioned horse-trading comes into play 'cause chew is like toilet paper… when its in short supply it might as well be <u>gold</u>. The sharp opportunist always packs in extra stock for such occasions.

At some point, you might be wondering if a single woman working in the hills with a bunch of wannabes might have found it tempting to indulge in some hanky panky? Answer: No I did not — for more than a dozen good reasons. Firstly, because my Daddy didn't raise no turnip. And secondly, because there is no faster way to screw up a job than to be messing around with the help. I wanted a job, not an adventure and besides, cowboy wannabes have a lot in common with musicians, whose reputations are well known. Different stage, different outfits and props, but it is a show nonetheless, and often without a whole lot of substance behind it. A girl who makes such transgressions in the hills can be assured that she will be *talked about* <u>throughout</u> the hills now and forever. The cowboy telegraph is said to be quicker and more scorching than lightning, and it never forgets. I sometimes overheard the guys regaling in tales of all the women who had chased them (they wish). After all, being lusted after by chicks was the single greatest reward of the wrangling profession for a lot of guys. To get themselves hired on to some guest ranch and be surrounded by adoring women — ahhh, that was the life. If a fella was blessed with a particularly fine set of buns, then a smart pair of chaps could only improve upon the back view. For the less fortunate, a well-placed sock would compensate on the front view. Don't be shocked — plenty of guys do it.

Next critical cowboy wannabe expression and a <u>must</u> <u>know</u>:

...this ain't ma first rodeo..."

Sounds simple, but it implies volumes. "This ain't ma first rodeo" denotes a certain background of experience, years of rough ridin' under the belt that defies words. Spoken correctly with a no-nonsense, matter of fact growl, it may effectively put an end to all doubt that you are the cowboy to end all cowboys. Beware, however, that if you then set off to the current task at hand (the one to which you have alluded a complete mastery) and make a complete and utter fool of yourself, you may want to find another outfit to work for. Else wise, you will want to substitute that saying for something like this:

"Yessir Howdy Bob Schucks, how high shall I jump?"

There is a fellow in Jackson who operated up his own little outfitter supply shop —a nice little place to pick up Dutch ovens and handy tools for the trail. This fellow had a lot invested in playing the part, and he dressed it up well. Right down to the combed mustache and good ole' boy accent. If you got him talking about his own experiences you would soon be rewarded with that magical phrase — *"this ain't ma first rodeo,"* and he knew just how to lay it on thick. Could be that he did have the skills and trail time to back it up (I am certainly not one to talk) however I heard it somewhere on the wind that he landed from California, and I have laughed about it ever since.

Being a wrangler or a wannabe or camp cook is not for everybody. Like mw, some of us try it out for a while and it either fits or it doesn't. I never tried to pretend I was anything but myself. In truth, I could not handle the whole job, but parts of it I did do well. Mainly, I could not have embraced a life around a bunch of guys whom I did not relate to, and this was not my home.

But like window shopping, it is fun to take in the view once in awhile, maybe even try something on, whether it is meant to be yours — or not. My years of camp cooking were much shorter than the memories that persist, like that potent smell of bacon grease and bug dope deeply infused into my hat.

If you are reading this, snug in some easy chair in some urban place, you might be glad of where you are. Or you might be curious. If so, perhaps you will venture out West some day. One cannot accurately describe how glorious that country is — or how it seems to go on forever. Sometimes the stars feel so close you might pluck one for yourself. Along the way a subtle thing may happen — that your view of the world might shift and you find an undiscovered aspect of yourself. The West tends to fill a place we did not realize was empty and there are those who wander out West and never wander back.

If you fancy the idea of wearing the trappings of a wannabe for a while, then perhaps I have offered you a few valuable tips on where to start. If nothing else, you will recognize the species when you see it.

WANNABEANS*

Lighter and sweeter than the regular cowboy beans, but theyget the job done.

1 lb.	yellow eye beans
½ tsp.	baking soda
½ C.	sugar
3 T.	molasses
1 tsp.	powdered ginger
1 T.	maple syrup
1 tsp.	prepared mustard
¼ tsp.	thyme
1 T.	ketchup
½ stick	margarine or butter
2 tsp.	salt
1/8 tsp.	pepper
¼ tsp.	parsley flakes

Soak beans overnight in cold water.

In the morning drain the beans, add new water and parboil. When the water comes to a boil add the soda and skim off the foam. Beans have boiled long enough if the skins split when you blow on them. Drain, put beans in pot or covered casserole and add the remaining ingredients and enough water to cover.

Bake several hours at 275°F degrees. Check often and add water as needed.

*A bean, by any other name brings about the same reaction. This is another recipe from my Ma's favorites… though she has her own name for them.

CHAPTER IV

THE HELL OF THE ROOT RANCH

THE FLYING RESORTS

The Frank Church Wilderness of No Return is nestled in the heart of Idaho. Like a scattering of rare pearls in the midst of all this wild country are a few remaining private ranches and old air strips, protected by the Grandfather Act, which allows them to exist. The Flying B and the Root Ranch are two such entities, which doubtless raise the ire of those who would like to see such protection revoked. Nonetheless, business at the ranches has continued for many years, and the tiny percent of mankind who actually get to visit paradise remain thankful for this small favor. *(I am somewhat puzzled by this movement to eradicate man, as if he never existed, from all the beautiful places in our country... take pictures while you can.)*

I spent only a few weeks helping out in the kitchen at the Flying B, while waiting for winter to clear out of the high country so I could start up at the Root Ranch. The Flying B is the largest ranch owned by the Flying Resort Ranches out of Salmon, Idaho. Both ranches are maintained by a membership of over 150 owners, many of who own small airplanes. Other folks visit by way of chartered flight, and still others stop in for meals and beer via river raft on the beautiful Middle Salmon River, which runs right past the Flying B. However you may arrive, visitors are welcomed at both ranches, though certain restrictions apply and you may wish to inquire of them prior to landing.

The Flying B features a rustic old lodge serving three big meals per day, and individual cabins with linen and maid service, etc. This ranch offers electricity produced by hydropower from a nearby creek; a well-seasoned herd of horses maintained for those who like to trail ride; and of course target and skeet shooting and fishing for the outdoorsman. In the summer, the foothills offer countless trails to explore and hike. In the fall, both ranches are available for hunting. For the feebleminded, there are always the clouds.

My personal favorite was to ride up river from the Flying B and follow a small creek to the hot spring for a late afternoon soak (be ever so mindful of poison ivy). Along the way was an old Mormon homestead, now in the clutches of the Forest Service. Odd to imagine how folks survived deep in the wilderness all those years ago. It must have been a wild, hard life though game and fish must have been plentiful. Once I relocated to the Root Ranch, I really missed that old hot spring. One thing I did not miss, besides the poison ivy, was that kitchen full of gossiping women, half of whom seemed to be at perpetual odds with the other — while vying for the few available men with a pulse. Oy! I soon dubbed the ranch as *The Flying Bullshit* and looked forward to escaping.

The Root Ranch is the smaller of the two ranches. It offers a more modest cook building where meals are prepared and served three times per day, along with a cozy lodge overlooking high foothills, rolling meadows and a creek which meanders through it. Guest cabins are stripped down by comparison, offering simple bunks and mattresses for guests to roll out their own sleeping bags or bedding. Outhouses are located in the back — single-holers. Modern plumbing and showers are located in the lodge. Most all conveniences are propane fueled as electricity is a rare commodity available only on laundry days and special occasions. One used to spot elk, moose and deer at the creek bottom below the lodge and throughout the ranch at different times of the season, though I hear this has changed since the reintroduction of the wolf. At night, wolf howls echo through the mountains, and the stars are clear and bright far away from city lights. The Root Ranch is rumored to have been used as a hideout for horse wrassling in the old days. Check out the narrow gun sites in the old rough hewn barn, which were used for that purpose. Not to worry — the Ranch is markedly quieter nowadays and it is a good place to be at peace with yourself.

During early season at the Root Ranch, Youth Camp is held where 25 kids enjoy a week of guided events such as camping and hiking, an overnight pack trip, target practicing, skeet shooting, archery, a very creative obstacle course, games and such. A week when the ranch is filled with laughter. Guaranteed, there is always a waiting list for this coveted event.

During June, the Root Ranch offers a wilderness packer course when young hopefuls spend a month learning to handle and pack horses, shoe horses, navigate and guide in the wilderness, call in game, and dress out game, etc. This was a month filled with humor and cussing. Come fall, it is the usual hunting season. I was long gone by then, so you will have to draw upon your imagination. I do suspect that far more booty is bagged at the poker table, than was ever bagged at the hunt.

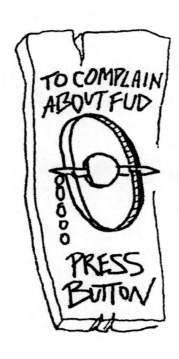

FLYING FERDINAND'S MARINATED ROAST

Flying Ferdinand is the indomitable manager of not one but several guest ranches, the names of which shall remain unmentioned, and this recipe is proof that even the toughest piece of meat can be transformed into a virtual delicacy. Use this marinade on your favorite roast.

1 C.	soy sauce
½ C.	brown sugar
½ clove	garlic, crushed
½ tsp.	ginger root powder
1 T.	Worcestershire Sauce
¼ C.	vegetable oil
½ tsp.	course black pepper

Sprinkle liberally with meat tenderizer (Adolph's w/papaya enzymes is my personal favorite) and pierce heavily with fork. Turn every few hours and marinate overnight. Broil or grill as desired.

THE GAS MAN

If only I had saved some of my old journals – that way, I would be able to account for some of the names of the characters. This story is about a fellow (I will call him "The Gas Man") who worked for the local gas company in Salmon, Idaho. Every spring, the boss would fly the Gas Man into the Root Ranch so he could service all the propane appliances. We would feed him, put him up in a nice cabin for the night, and as a bonus, he would get to come back in the fall during hunting season — an agreeable deal all the way around.

But winter was not letting go of her mountains easily that year (1996) and we had been stalled a good three weeks getting into the ranch. On this very night in May it was snowing bitterly. I had toughed it out until then, not wanting to turn on the propane heater in my cabin. But when the snow flew I thought, hell, — why not? If I got into trouble I knew whom to call. So I began fiddling with the control (which was barely visible in my quaint, dark, sans-electric cabin). Best intentions aside, the heater was an ancient, leaky wall unit, and I managed little more than to put out the pilot light. I did not find the thermostat knob, which was hidden around the corner, but I could discern that I was about to get into trouble. I knocked on Mr. Gas Man's door and asked if he minded lending a hand, pretty please? It is important to note that I DID explain I had been playing with the knobs, and that the pilot was out. He said he would be happy to help even so.

Once back at my cabin, the Gas Man hunkered down on the floor, peered at the works with his flashlight, and lit a match. By firelight, he looked as innocent as a babe. **kaBOOOOOM!** A tube of flame shot straight out from the heater and hit the Gas Man square in the face. Amazingly, he never let out a squeak. I was mortified — praying he had not been hurt. Since the Gas Man was wearing a visor cap and had placed a hand over his face, I could not be certain. I squeaked, *"Are you OK?"* — silence. Then the Gas Man muttered, *"Well — that takes care of THAT mustache."*

Honest, I tried to hold it in, I did. But one look at his mustache, all tattered and burnt, and I just could not. The more I imagined it, the more I laughed until finally I had to leave. Surprisingly, he was still willing to approach the devil heater again.

For the second time, the Gas Man hunkered down on the floor, peered into the works and trustingly lit a match. This time, he looked a bit more wary, kind of like a guy what's been burnt by love or something.

kaBOOOOM! For the second time, a tube of flame shot straight out and hit the Gas Man in the face. By now, I could not begin to imitate composure. A group of people had heard the explosion and come to investigate. They found him collecting scraps of mustache, and me, clinging to the side of the cabin and laughing so hard that I could neither stand nor talk. No point in trying to make apologies either. Yes, that flame had given the Gas Man a helluva wake-up call, and I went so far as to quip *"Gee, you musta' thought you had a telephone line straight to HELL! Hello?* **KaBOOOM!"** Bahahahahaha!

Undaunted, the Gas Man lit the heater (third time being a charm) and at my insistence, assured me that he was indeed all right (liar). He allowed as he was inclined to forgive me for laughing in the face of tragedy; however, I now owed him **TWO** home baked apple pies upon his return in the fall. With that, he disappeared into the kitchen to shave the remains of his mustache by flashlight and more than likely give it a decent burial.

Can you imagine what they must have said in town when the Gas Man returned without his mustache? Indeed, his face was pink with telltale burns. He could have made up some pretty incriminating stories about that crazy cook at the Root Ranch. Doesn't take much to get something started in a small town — especially in a place like Salmon where intrigue and scandal are common. (That's a nice way of saying there was a certain tendency towards promiscuity.)

I will never know, because I did not stick around long enough to pay that debt. The long hours had caught up with me, and I was faced with a severe case of burnout. Honest, I did mean to square up about the pies, and I did feel a twinge of guilt at the time of my premature departure, and very nearly sent in some frozen ones to suffice.

Maybe it is better I was gone when he returned? What's that old saying about "once burnt, twice shy?" Had he not gotten himself burnt TWICE? It may just be that my leaving saved him further pain and embarrassment. Yes, I do believe that some things are just not meant to be, and that it is important to know when to "git."

And besides, what would I do for an encore?

MOM'S APPLE CRISP or STUFFED APPLES*

This recipe is dedicated to the Gas Man, who suffered greatly in the line of fire and went without due compensation. Unfortunately, I never caught the knack of making piecrusts.

4 C.	apples, peeled, cored, sliced
2/3 C.	brown sugar, packed
½ C.	flour
½ C.	rolled oats
1 tsp.	cinnamon
1 tsp.	nutmeg
6 T.	soft butter

Place apples in greased 9x9 pan. Mix above ingredients and crumble over top of apples. Bake for 30-35 minutes at 375°F. Let cool for 15 minutes or so and serve with ice cream. Serves six. Double batch as needed.

I have also used this recipe to bake individual apples. Wash and core apple (Macintosh or Cortland work well). Fill core with crisp mixture and bake in pan with 1/2 cup of water, same time and temperature.

*This is my all-time favorite of Ma's cooking collection, and though I never heard of her stuffing it... undoubtedly she was tempted at times.

THE GIRLS

There are all kinds of folk in the backcountry and in the summertime, the mountains are crawling with people who find some way to stay for the season. In the midst of all the various forms of recreation (pack trips, fishing, horseback, backpack, wolf expeditions, white water rafting, kayaking, mountain climbing, biking, hunting) are the forest service personnel who maintain discipline, and the forest service trail crews who maintain the trails. That summer the Root Ranch was visited by two fine young women who had proudly signed up for the Cold Meadows Trail Crew. They might have been the ONLY trail crew — I cannot recall. But you would never have guessed, had you seen them on a street somewhere, that those two skinny girls would spend their whole summer cutting trees with a two-man saw and hauling them off trail. Add to the fact that they would wander throughout backcountry with provisions and tents on their backs – country inhabited by wolves, bears and mountain lions, not to mention a healthy population of flying pests such as mosquitoes and horseflies, all competing for a taste of you. But these were no ordinary girls, and woe to man or beast that underestimated them.

First of all the sheer smell that preceded them (if you happened to be down wind) was enough to knock you over. The girls worked up a hard sweat every day, and they wore it proud. I offered hot showers at the ranch many times, but they always politely declined. Seemed like it was a rite of passage, and besides, I suspect it kept the bugs away. One thing the girls did enjoy was dinner at the ranch from time to time. Strict vegetarians, they partook only of salads, vegetables and breads. The girls did develop a particular fondness for Beer Bread (featured in this collection of writing), so I shared the recipe. I believe they developed their own variation using a dark beer with wheat flour and honey.

When it came time for the Packer's Guide program, seven men from varying backgrounds and personalities inhabited the Root Ranch for 30 days. Besides yours truly, there were no women — which made the Cold Meadows Trail Crew look mighty attractive even with the aforementioned traits. One night a couple of the guys stowed some beer in their pockets and meandered down the meadow and across the creek to the girls' campsite. I could have told the guys they were wasting their time, and you would think they would have known better. The young ladies were practicing feminists and no redneck bumpkin would have attracted their interest on even the best day. I can just imagine what they must have thought when they spotted the guys coming. In any event, it was the last time the guys wasted any beer on the girls.

Personally I do not knock feminism, and Lord knows I have had my own issues with men — but I have long since moved beyond getting uppity if a man called me a *girl*, or *darlin,'* or *sweetheart*, or *sugar* or what have you. Out West, such things are terms of endearment, and I like them. In fact, I often use these terms myself and I mean it the same way — no offense or slight intended. During some of these jobs I would have given <u>anything</u> for such small kindnesses. With that foundation, you might understand how I felt, learning that the girls had been somewhat peeved that I called them "the girls." I would see them coming up the meadow and holler out, "Hey Girls, come join us for dinner!" I guess they got used to it, and eventually found me somewhat humorous — which was why they let me in on the secret. While I tend not to question another's beliefs, I did take the opportunity to share a few thoughts on the matter.

"Girls — you know I mean no offense when I call you that — but let me tell you why. Firstly, it is important to know where you are. Secondly, it is important to know that words cannot hit your 'buttons,' unless you <u>have</u> them. At this age, words are so important to you — you are learning to articulate your world and you seek respect. But at some point, we begin to look beyond words. We look at who we are, and who we know our selves to be —— regardless of words or what others may think. You can choose to react when a man calls you 'darlin' or 'girl' — yes you can twist right off and either give him a good show, or alienate him, depending upon his own private intent, or lack thereof. Or you can save your energy and your words for when something really important comes up —— for those moments when you would like to be heard and respected for your beliefs. 'Reacting' to words changes nothing — not that man who has grown up with those forms of expressions all his life, and who will use them long after you are gone. And not you, who have not yet learned to look beyond the words."

The girls looked at each other, and back at me. I never knew if they agreed with what I said, which really did not matter, but I suspect it gave them something to think on for a spell.

Summer moved along with its oppressive heat, and soon enough, I knew it was time for me to leave the ranch. Those long hours of cooking were eroding my sense of sanity, and my own internal buttons were raw and ripe for the pushing. The Girls stopped by for a visit, and were sorry to hear the news. Upon departing they asked if I would take their picture for old time's sake? I said, "*Sure! Back yourself on up against the* **Horn Wall**" (that rustic view of the old barn that was covered with old deer and elk antlers, and which made an excellent backdrop.) One of the old timers heard me and snorted so hard he nearly blew out his chew. I laughed and took their picture — arm in arm, smiling in the sun at that special moment in their lives. I wonder where they are now? I wonder what they think when they look back on those times? Carin & Chappell gave me a comical homemade card, thanking me so much for all the fine food and my generosity. It said that they enjoyed visiting the Root Ranch and talking with me — wishing me luck on my next adventure…they also wished me peace.

It does not get any better than that.

TOSSED GREENS WITH MANDARIN*

In this place, it is only fitting that a "treehuggar special" be featured. No wranglers, cowboys or other forms of wildlife were harmed in the making of this salad.

1 can	Mandarin orange, drained
1 head	romaine lettuce, washed & dried
1 bunch	green onions, chopped w/greens
¾ stalks	celery, chopped

Top with:

1	avocado, peeled and cubed
	sugared almonds slices

SWEET & SOUR DRESSING

¼ C.	vegetable oil
2 T.	sugar
2 T.	vinegar
1 T.	snipped parsley
½ tsp.	salt
	dash of pepper
	dash of red pepper sauce

Toss greens in a large bowl and chill. Toss in dressing when ready to serve and top with avocado. Sugared almonds slices may be served on the side or on top. (To sugar almond slices, heat pan on medium high, stir almonds constantly, until lightly browned. Remove from heat and sprinkle with sugar and let cool.)

*This recipe was shared by a summer guest – I believe the Girls would approve.

CAPTAIN BLOWHARD

Feature this: An average stubby middle-aged man, white hair, overgrown mustache, and even further overgrown belly, blue jeans that hang precariously under the aforementioned belly, cowboy boots, and a cocky little man stature as he barrels through your kitchen like Blackbeard himself has landed. Meet Captain Blowhard. I first became acquainted with the old bag of wind as he was, in fact, blustering through my kitchen like an old hurricane that had not yet learned how to blow itself out. Many times I wished he would... blow himself out. Anyways, this fellow was a one-time foreman at the Root Ranch. I believe they were desperate that year, and I got the impression that it had not worked out so well. There was some rumor of a mutiny. Nonetheless, Captain Blowhard was in full form, and he was intent on letting me know just who was the captain of this here ship.

Captain Blowhard had lined himself up as the head instructor for the fledgling Packer Training course — probably cause nobody else wanted the pleasure, and most likely because he came cheap. I wish someone had warned me; I would have stocked extra bologna. The guide program was due to start within days and Captain B was making preliminary rounds — just long enough to decide he did not like me it seemed. Captain B then made a quick trip back to the Flying B to gather cleaning supplies, where he apparently spouted off to the head cook (who was his cousin) that *he would soon have that cook at the Root Ranch on her <u>hands</u> and <u>knees</u>, scrubbing that floor till it was spotless!* Folks, that floor had suffered ground in dirt and gravel for at least 20 years of male inhabitation, and there was as much chance of it getting spotless, as there was of the Queen Mother scrubbing it. Captain B did not realize I had a friend working at the Flying B. Thus, he would pay for his bit of arrogance more than a few times that summer.

One day, Captain Blowhard and the boys brought horses up from the Flying B — which entailed two days of hard riding through snow-covered mountains and raging spring rivers. (I was only too glad to have missed it, and only narrowly at that.) Unbeknownst to me, Little Joe was coming down with a sore throat. Instead of asking nicely, Captain B bellowed *"Would someone git' movin' and BRAnnnNG something for his throat!"* Since I was the only *someone* within earshot, I supposed he was yelling at me? I promptly offered to take care of Little Joe's throat by way of throttling it. And the Captain's too, if he'd like. The man sure knew how to make an impression.

If there was one thing that peeved Captain B, (other than hardheaded women) it was puny slices of meat in his sandwich, or puny thin pork chops on his dinner plate. (Had he been able to peer over his belly, I believe Captain B would have been slightly peeved at what the good Lord gave him as well.) It mattered not how well you prepared the meal or how many pork chops were piled on his plate – if they were thin, he commenced to whining and carrying on. My provision of bologna came by way of an immense meat tube, so after considerable whining I dutifully cut thicker slices to pacify Captain B. Unappeased, he continued to fuss and complain, until one day I sliced that bologna about two inches thick and slapped it between two slices of bread for his sandwich. I figured he might blow his lid, realizing that I was mocking him. Turned out that was exactly the way he liked it. As the saying goes – *you are what you eat.*

Captain Blowhard prided himself on being a sore spot in my side, and liked to do so in front of an audience whenever possible. One evening he bellowed at me to *get outta his way* as he was trying to make for the chow line. (Not like he was in danger of wasting away or nothing.) I piped up and said, *"Ya know... I believe it is time you had your very own special seat."* Captain B puffed up and drawled *"Wellllll Ahhh'd like that!"* (Like it's just about time you came around Little Missy?) I continued, *"Yes indeed, I can just see it now...your special seat will* *be sculpted out of the very **finest** white porcelain.*" Captain B's face turned scarlet red as the dining room (filled with HIS students) erupted with laughter. I believe that was the last time he went for the public humiliation tactic.

It was not long before Captain Blowhard began needling and prodding for me to put some elbow grease to that floor — like I hadn't been expecting it? But seeing as how I was averaging around 13 hours per day in that kitchen, 3 meals per day, 7 days per week, I mainly ignored the little pest. Kind of like a mosquito bite — I mused that if someone rubbed some calamine lotion on him, he might go away. Nothing doing. Eventually I had enough haranguing and Captain B got some of my religion — which was, *any day of the week he thought that floor needed some scrubbing he was more than welcomed to have at it!* In fact, considering the hours I was working, and for the relatively little I was being compensated, he was perilously close to having my job. That boy's mama raised her a fool —

Following that episode, Captain Blowhard still had plenty to say for he was the type that never would shut up. However he found other ears to bestow it upon and I was spared the pleasure. Years later, I can guarantee you that floor is no whiter, and without doubt, Captain B is not one whit wiser.

Captain Blowhard's Throne

JERK CHICKEN

Without further ado, and with no explanation required … we give you Jerk Chicken!

MARINADE

2-3	jalapenos, seeded
1 T.	molasses
1 T.	soy sauce
1 T.	Worcestershire sauce
1	lime, juice and grated peel
1 tsp.	brown sugar
4 tsp.	butter, softened
3	green onions/scallions, chopped
3 cloves	garlic, peeled & sliced thinly
¼ tsp.	black pepper
1 tsp.	salt
2 tsp.	ground cinnamon
2 tsp.	allspice
1 T.	fresh ginger, peeled & sliced thinly
1/3 C.	cider vinegar

Combine all jerk season ingredients in a food processor or blender. Blend until smooth.

1 4-5 lb.	chicken
1 pc.	ginger (thumb-sized) peeled and sliced thinly
1 head	garlic, cut in half
1	lime, cut in quarters
1	jalapeno, halved lengthwise

Adjust oven rack to center of oven and preheat to 450°F. Rinse and dry the chicken; massage ½ of the jerk seasoning all over the chicken, under the breast skin and inside the cavity. Place the ginger, garlic, lime and chile inside the cavity and close by tying the ends of the drumsticks together loosely.

Place chicken with the breast-side down on an oiled rack over a roasting pan; roast for 30 minutes, brushing with pan juices and jerk seasoning every 10 minutes or so. If pan juices sizzle too loudly or begin to smoke, add ½ cup of water to the pan.

Flip the chicken breast-side up and reduce oven temperature to 350°F. Continue roasting an additional hour, basting frequently. Chicken is done when skin is crisp and brown and the drumsticks feel loose. A meat thermometer inserted into the thick part of the thigh nearest the body should register from 165°F - 175°F. Transfer to a platter or carving board and let rest for 15-20 minutes before serving.

In the meantime, transfer the pan juices to a small saucepan and skim off the fat. Remove the garlic and chile from the cavity, chop finely and combine with pan juices. Heat to a simmer, and serve alongside chicken.

WILL: THE OTHER WHITE MEAT

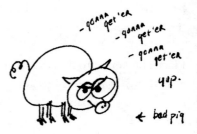

- gonna get 'er
- gonna get 'er
- gonna get 'er

yup.

← bad pig

It is somewhat distressing having to account for some of these unseemly characters. This is starting to sound more like the battle of the sexes — which it was — though I had not intended it to be. But a woman cannot throw herself into a man's world and expect any less, so here is another one that is sure to curl my Grandmother's toes.

During the slow season, the Root Ranch did what many other self-respecting outfits have done. They farmed themselves out as a packer/guide training facility. Thus, seven unsuspecting men were delivered unto the ranch one morning with dreams of adventure, expecting to depart in 30 days with the right to call themselves "wilderness packers and guides." Ideally, they would then find a job, and get paid for going out to play in the woods. In any event, the boys were committed to stay the duration, because the plane departed before they had time for second thoughts. It is about an 60-mile walk out otherwise.

On that very first day, the first hour in fact, one student whose name was Will, made his first and lasting impression by generously offering me a big $20 to do his laundry for the month. I said I would forgive that first offense and let him live. <u>Lesson One</u>: Never mess with the cook.

That evening, we were all visiting on the stoop when I made an observation that turned out to be fairly accurate. One of the fellows asked how I knew that? I guessed I just had a way of looking at people that tells me who they are. Will piped up, *"OhYEA? Why don't you read ME?"*

All right. But are you sure you want me to say it? Cause it comes out just like I hear it. He thought hard for a minute, and said yes. I hesitated, then said, "*Forgive me, but YOU a pussy hound — devoted to a life of pursuing the opposite sex. When you aren't chasing it, you are thinking about it — always trying to figure a way to catch a piece. Not that you want to keep it for long — you just want to play with it for a few minutes. Now there is nothing wrong with this if it is who you are, and who you want to be. Just understand that not many woman find such qualities attractive in a man.*"

The other fellows were somewhat aghast, as if expecting him to come unhinged. But Will thought on it a spell, and after what appeared to be an uncomfortable millisecond, agreed that I was right. Seemed he had not thought of himself in that light — but danged if it did not fit.

Unfortunately, my observation turned out to be all too prophetic and Will must have regarded that first event as foreplay, because for the next four weeks I could not rid myself of him. I was not flattered — this was not a man of any distinguishable character. The raw fact of the matter was that I was the only woman around; not counting the livestock and Will was in hot pursuit. Lord have mercy upon my bones. He would hang around the kitchen trying just about any angle he could dream up: from Mr. Sensitive, Mr. Helpful, Mr. Funny, Mr. Raunchy, and finally Mr. Why Don't You Just Give It Up So You Can Git Rid of Me. I know the other guys made fun of him. And I told him to run along on more than one occasion. In turn, I tried just about everything I could dream up to discourage him, from Miss Humor Him, Miss Teflon, Miss Tolerant, Miss Testy and finally Miss Say Hello To My French Knife and So Long to Your Private Parts. You would think he might get the hint and QUIT.

One afternoon, I stepped out the back door to throw some trash in the burn barrel, when someone yelled, "**Don't Look!**" I shrugged and returned to the kitchen. Turns out Will had been relieving himself behind a nearby laundry shack. Probably spying on me in the process, which didn't warm my heart any — and Lord knows what <u>else</u> he might have been doing back there.

Will stepped into the kitchen, making a big show of gettin' hisself back together and announced in his gravely smoker's voice, "*That was close — I was takin' a leak, and you almost SAW IT!*"

SAW IT? Oh please. I couldn't resist saying "*Honey, that ain't NOTHIN' I haven't seen before,*" thinking a little sharp humor might put an end to this foolishness. (Did I tell you I attended art school, and that we drew naked people regularly?)

Undaunted, Will purred, "*Well ya haven't seen THIS one, 'cause if ya had, you might just go CRAZY!* (Whoa HO! That's a new one!)

> ME: "*Oh REALLY … and what would you call THAT affliction — DICK FEVER?*"
>
> WILL: "**GAWD!!!** *No one's ever accused YOU of being SHY!*"
>
> ME: "*Nope. Not lately.*"

Will visibly recoiled with disgust and I deluded myself that I might finally be free of this unending, UNwanted nuisance. It had been several weeks now, there was no one to step in and intervene and I had really had the limit. Will slunk out the back door as I resumed the task of preparing dinner. I was still laughing when one of the other fellows stopped in soon after. He had a good sense of humor and I did not see any harm in sharing the laugh. Apparently, he then proceeded to tease Will in front of the boys, adding further insult to the injury. Now I would have my peace and quiet for sure!

That evening, I headed out of the kitchen for a hike in the surrounding mountains. This was my daily salvation – to go bushwhacking and exploring elk runs, to swim in the creek and soothe the aches from a long, tiring day, and to feel that I had some worthwhile reason for being in this place. The country was beautiful, but the job was surely a facet of hell. Inevitably, I would be gone for hours, returning to the ranch well after dark.

On this particular night, as I returned via the wooded path bordering the pasture, I listened to the usual elk herd in the meadow, only they were agitated and sounding alarm. Elk babies were chirping, and soon the whole herd was bolting through the trees around me so close that I wondered if I was going to get flattened. You may never realize how intensely powerful elk are until you get caught in the middle of a stampede — although the chances of this happening are unlikely. Usually they run the other way.

I arrived at the pasture in one piece only to find the peculiar sight of the horses jumping over the fence one by one. Now this was odd. Something must really be spooking the animals to cause them to act this way — most likely a mountain lion, bear, or a wolf as we had all three predators in this country. I walked across the last long stretch of open pasture and headed to bed chuckling – had to feel sorry for whoever got wrangle duty the next morning. Those boys would surely be hatin' life whilst searching for horses that were scattered for miles. Furthermore, it was wrangler tradition that they would not be allowed to come in for breakfast until every horse was corralled. This is just one of those outfitter rules that you may as well learn from the start.

Sure enough, the unhappy wranglers were late for breakfast that morning. The horses had indeed roamed wide and far, and as far as they could see, the program brochure had not said <u>anything</u> about working on an empty stomach. As the boys commiserated with the group (secretly proud as they no doubt sprouted chest hairs at that very moment), I recounted what I had seen coming back from my hike. *What had scared the animals so?* Just then, the fellow to whom I had confided about Will piped up in a high mocking tone, *"It was **Will**, he was takin' a leak, and they **SAW IT!**"* The whole room erupted in laughter. Will sat glowering while I laughed too. I did not generally go for public humiliation, but if it cooled his not so romantic notions, it was worth it. He had to admit, he was warned, repeatedly, to go find someone else to pester. Just my luck, we had no sheep.

You might be thinking that this was the last of it, but it was not. However, I will exercise the liberty of skipping over unpleasantries. It is enough to say that Will's humor took a turn to the dark side from that time on. Will was not a graceful loser. Concurrently, I was not a willing participant.

One day Will was bragging about his ways with women, calling himself "The Two-Minute Man" like it was something to be proud of. The guys proceeded to give him a rash of grief, to which he retorted, "*HEY, I never heard no complaints from the ladies.*" "*Of course not,* I quipped, *that would have taken* **three** *minutes.*" The boys roared with laughter.

Suffice to say; when it was time for them to leave, I was most delighted. Will, while not acting as overtly aggressive, did continue to make a pest of himself. I counted him as no more annoying than the horseflies at that time of year and just bided my time, figuring he would get his in the end. Nothing could have been closer to the truth.

To conclude the guide program, the instructors arranged a final review session on the "joys of horseshoeing." Will was working on the back end of his horse when the tail went up. Everybody yelled *git out of the Waaay* — but it was too late. Will got plastered and the boys enjoyed the show immensely. Will slunk into the kitchen with an interesting new design on his shirt (kind of like that "I ran into Tammy Faye" number) and was disgusted to find sympathy lacking in my department as well. Oh please — isn't it time for you to leave!

During the last few days, when all the guys were wearing their best happy faces, hopeful of being offered a job at the ranch, I was horrified to hear that Will was being considered because better prospects had declined. But why? He was worthless with horses, nobody liked him, and his skills as a guide — well I just could not imagine they amounted to much. Besides, he had no heart and cared little about life in general. But they offered him the job anyway. Will made special point of saying that he would have two whole additional months to pursue me, in which time he felt certain that he would succeed. Oh joy. Will was due back in three weeks — just in time for the start of hunting season. I had a feeling the "season" was on me.

When one realizes that I was averaging nearly 90 hours per week in the kitchen with a whopping three days off at the end of each month, during which time I struggled to gather enough beans to endure the next month, one might assume that additional sources of stress were unwelcomed. A live-in pest like Will was definitely less than welcomed and only added to my definition of hell, which at this point is anything that requires cooking for a living.

Years ago, this had been a two-person job — that is, until some cantankerous old crone had signed on and thrown everybody out of her kitchen. I imagine the shareholders liked the bottom line savings — so from then on, it was a one-pony show. Several months into the job, I was already spent and could not conceive of lasting another two to three more months, no matter how I tried. It was time to talk with the boss, for if he failed to find a replacement fool, there would surely be an embarrassing public meltdown by yours truly. A very nice lady was found; I spent a week helping her make the transition, and then I flew out, never to return. (That wilderness was aptly named.)

My decision to leave had little to do with Will. I am tougher than that — though I was getting tired of being tough. Admittedly, I got a good chuckle at the thought of his returning with anticipation, only to find that I had escaped. The woman who replaced me was an older, no-nonsense kind of female, and I figured she would handle him right quick. I dare say she likely did a better job than I, on both counts. Regardless, Will, who I had come to regard as "The Other White Meat," was no longer my problem.

Oh yes, there is a God.

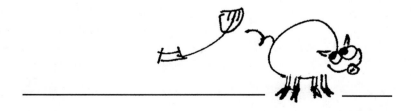

ROAST PORK* (in honor of Will)

1   pork loin or roast

        white wine (Chablis or Chardonnay)
        Season-All seasoning
        poultry seasoning blend
        rosemary powder

Place roast in pan, pour white wine over it. Coat with Season-All and poultry seasoning blend. Sprinkle heavily with rosemary powder and pepper, if desired.

Cover roast and bake at 350°F for approximately 2-2 ½ hours if small roast, 3-3 ½ if large. Check temp using meat thermometer and remove at 170°F.

Drain broth into saucepan and return roast to oven, uncovered, to brown off.

CREAM SAUCE

Boil broth; add 1 tsp. rosemary powder and 1 tsp. granulated onion. Reduce heat and add 1 C. Half and Half or cream. Bring to boil, thicken with flour as needed. Pour over roast or serve on the side. Don't forget the applesauce!

*Recipe a long-time favorite at Coulter Lake Guest Ranch.

HONEY BARBEQUE RIBS

This is a personal recipe inspired by another character… I think Will needs a little honey to sweeten him up, and another good ribbing cannot hurt!

2-3	country style pork ribs per person (trimmed of fat)

SAUCE

4	cloves garlic, minced
6	scallions/green onions w/tops, washed & chopped
1	onion, chopped fine
½	green pepper, chopped fine
1 sm. can	green chilies or 2 fresh, chopped fine
½	jalapeno, chopped fine
1 sm. can	crushed tomato
1 sm. can	tomato paste
1 tsp.	grated orange peel
1-16 oz.	beer (optional)
1 tsp.	fennel
1 tsp.	rosemary
1 tsp.	garlic powder
1 tsp.	onion powder
¼ tsp.	dry mustard powder
2 tsp.	basil
2 tsp.	thyme
1 tsp.	black pepper
1 C.	honey
½ C.	molasses
	soy sauce or tamari

Sauté garlic, onion, green pepper, chilies and jalapeno in olive oil until onions are clear. Add crushed and paste tomato and grated orange peel. Dilute with water or beer and simmer to desired thickness. Add spices, continue simmering. Sweeten with honey & molasses. Add soy sauce or tamari to balance flavor as needed. Simmer another few minutes.

Place ribs in greased pan, sear in hot oven (475-500°F) until lightly browned. Pour off fat. Then cover generously with sauce, add water to hydrate some and bake 2 hours until tender. Rehydrate as needed.

MA'S BLT POTATO SALAD

2	hard cooked eggs
	(separate yolks and mash with fork, save whites)
1 C.	mayonnaise
¼ C.	sour cream
2 tsp.	vinegar
½ tsp.	dried Italian seasoning
½ tsp.	ground pepper
3 med.	potatoes (pre-cooked just firm, cooled & cubed)
8	cherry tomatoes (cut in halves)
6 slices	cooked bacon (crumbled)
½ C.	onion, chopped fine
	or powdered onion if preferred.

Mix eggs, mayo, sour cream, vinegar and seasonings in a bowl. Add cubed potato and cut up cooked egg whites. Toss in remaining ingredients and chill.

CHAPTER V

Moose Stories and Other Nonsense

MOOSEY DOES THE WATOOSEY

I remember a few old moose stories from Chuck Thornton's days as game warden. One winter a deranged cow moose was hanging out along the road and making it difficult for cars to pass or kids to get on their school bus. The locals tried everything to shoo her away but she stuck to that site and continued to make a "moosance" of herself. Finally Ranger Chuck shows up with his snow machine and attempts to drive her off, but she will have none of this. The snow banks are high and to engage her is to step into the arena, with very few alternatives for escape. In desperation, Chuck flings his coat on her head and quite miraculously it lands over her eyes with the sleeves fitting nicely over her large ears. Miss Moose commences to spin around and around, until she dislodges the offending particle from her head. Ranger Chuck is then treated to the spectacle of her performing the watoosey on his coat. You might not think that a large moose could get all four feet on one small coat, but she did, and she performed fine pirouettes with a vengeance.

T'weren't nothing left for a
decent burial.

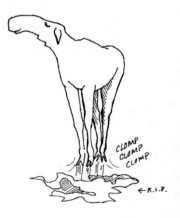

PARTING OF THE WATERS

Another time, Ranger Chuck, his dog and a friend were tromping through the woods when they encountered a hostile mama moose. Apparently the dog had taken off after her baby and she was frantic to locate it. Soon all three are running for their lives with mama moose in hot pursuit — Chuck says when you are in such a predicament as this, you vamoose and you do not look back. As it happened they were heading straight for a large pond. With an icy dip imminent, and few options available, wily Ranger Chuck grabs a hold of a small tree at the last second and swings off in the other direction. Following suit, the other fellow does so as well, and not a moment too soon. That hotheaded moose crashed full steam into the pond — a virtual parting of the waters I would imagine, allowing the men just enough time to scramble up a tree before she returned.

THE GREAT MOOSE DRIVE

My Daddy always said, "<u>Never</u> mess with a moose." I have always heeded those words; expanding them into a life philosophy simply stated, "Don't go looking for trouble." So imagine my distress when I realized what was about to take place?

It was fall into winter in Wyoming, meaning when you all are experiencing fall, we are heading into winter. Chuck's second moose hunter, the one with the smart mouth, had developed some great expectations about the trophy moose he intended to bag, mainly because we were fool enough to let on we had seen one. Chuck had something of a sweet deal with an old rancher who granted him permission to guide a hunter on his property that year, a beautiful ranch with a creek meandering through it and miles of tall willows providing prime moose habitat. In preparation for the hunt, Chuck and I went spotting one morning at dawn. Chuck could hardly believe his eyes on that fateful day when the king of moose stepped out of the mist. What an amazing beast he was, with a rack so broad he had to tilt it sideways to get through the trees. This was not your typical Shiras bull moose (common to the American West), this one tended towards the larger and more impressive Alaskan moose. Chuck was about spinning in his tracks, and so was the hunter once we blabbed about it. From then on, that hunter wanted his trophy so bad there would be no rest until he got it. When most other hunters might have taken a prudent afternoon break (during the hours when most hoofed beings are bedded down) this one had Chuck earning his keep and then some. But to no avail, which brings me to the point of this story.

After days of scouting and glassin', the big moose could not be found. As a final attempt to accommodate his hunter, Chuck proposed to perch him at a strategic overlook while we lined up and progressed through the bottom-land, end to end, calling out and pushing game ahead of us. This for the purposes of confirming what was hiding in there once and for all – did I tell you those willows were 20 foot or higher? A virtual maze of well-trod moose tunnels stretched out before us. I never heard of such a thing – driving for moose, and I was not too happy about participating. Especially with a potentially dissatisfied hunter watching from above, maybe having some fun with that scope on his rifle. I sure hope he liked my cooking.

"Chuck, I am not liking this idea of yours, and if I should get stomped by some moose, you are going to have some serious explaining to do for my Daddy." Duly noted, we headed into the willows. No doubt we looked like a bunch of deranged ants from the hunter's distant lookout, though I could not have cared less at the time. I was too busy beating my way through willows and thick underbrush, wondering what all was waiting for me on the other side? I could not decide what was worse – following the moose tunnels and getting a nice surprise, or getting hung up making my own way off-trail? I came to the creek and seeing no way around it, went right through it. (I rarely turn away from a good dip, and this looked to be the season's last one.) Maybe if I thrashed around enough I would scare a moose over Chuck's way and it would stomp him instead? Unless, of course, I happened to get Chuck's camera wet, in which case the moose would be the least of my concerns. Yes I bet that hunter was having himself a jolly good laugh up there. Next time I planned to switch places with him.

When we broke out of the willows and reached the end of our tour, I was both relieved and surprised. I neither saw nor heard one living creature, not one. Kind of wondered if we weren't but a bunch of fools until the hunter shared his version of the event. From his convenient location he had spotted 25 moose, only a handful of younger bulls, none being the Magnificent One. He did enjoy the rare spectacle of moose copulation – after all, tis' the season. Comically, the animals were not terribly concerned about our blundering racket through their sanctuary. They just shifted position and let us pass by unaware. I bet we looked stupid to them too.

As for the moose to end all mooses, he had apparently hightailed it over the hill to another drainage. That old bull knew he had been spotted, and he did not get to be that old by being stupid.

FIESTA MOOSE TURD BALLS*

Well, if you are going to go a'hunting after for moose, you might as well make a party of it!

1-2 lb.	ground moose meat
1-2 med.	onion, minced and divided
4 cloves	garlic, minced and divided
2 T.	cilantro, chopped and divided
1 T.	paprika
1 tsp.	salt
1/3 tsp.	ground black pepper
2	eggs, slightly beaten
¾ C.	uncooked rice (any brand)
	vegetable cooking spray
1-30 oz. can	tomato sauce
1 C.	beef broth
2	chipotle peppers, pickled
1½ T.	chili powder

Combine moose meat, 2 tablespoons onion, 1 clove garlic, 1 tablespoon cilantro, paprika, salt, pepper, eggs, and rice. Mix well and shape into small meatballs. Place in large baking dish coated with cooking spray. Combine tomato sauce, broth, remaining onion, peppers and chili powder, remaining garlic in blender jar. Cover and process until smooth. Put sauce in large skillet; cook over medium-high heat, stirring constantly 3-5 minutes. Pour sauce over meatballs and bake covered at 350° F degrees for 1 hour or until rice is tender. Sprinkle with remaining cilantro. Serve hot…

*Another recipe from Dennis Fisher's Wild Game Recipes at www.fishersnet.com. Copyright ©1995, 1996, 1997, 1998 by Dennis Fisher. Recipe received in a mass mailing of recipes, author is unknown

LARGE AND IN CHARGE

One summer, a mama moose and her calf took up residence at the Turpin Meadows Guest Ranch in Wyoming. For months she haunted the fields, lurked between cabins terrorizing the guests and crew without warning and making a general hazard of herself. Imagine how alarming it would be to saunter sleepily out of your cabin one morning and find yourself running for life with hot moose breath on your back in the next nano-second?

Well a certain wrangler (who later became an outfitter) set his sights on remedying the problem. He tried every little scheme imaginable to coax, cajole, and even trap that mama and calf with irresistible treats. But none of his ploys worked – seemed like she was determined to become a permanent installation, as well as a daily threat.

Finally, as a last ditch effort, our fearless wrangler saddled up his trusty horse and tore out bright and early after the pair, determined to drive them out for good. The guests, who had just seated themselves in the dining room for breakfast, were treated to the rare and breathtaking view of mama and her

baby, bolting past the big picture window with the wrangler in hot pursuit. Moments later, however, the tables were turned when those same guest witnessed that same wrangler riding hell bent for leather, with mama moose LARGE and IN CHARGE on his tail. I believe this merits a seat in the wrangler hall of fame, if ever there was such a thing, for goofiest wrangler moment.

And though the event no doubt made a lasting impression on the guests (I bet they still laugh about it to this day) it did not deter the young and impressionable miss, who would later become Mrs. Wrangler. I would pity the woman, but you cannot say she didn't get an eyeful.

THE DEVIL MOOSE

Thirty miles north of Turpin Meadows Ranch into the Bridger-Teton Wilderness, just shy of the southeast Yellowstone border is an old log cabin, now utilized as a ranger station. Glorious broad meadows and wetlands filled with wildflowers in bloom, the Yellowstone River winding by and clear blue skies above. One day several wranglers and myself were standing near the water's edge visiting with the local volunteer ranger and his wife when we spotted a mama moose and her young calf playing along the willows, headed straight in our direction and closing in. Mrs. Volunteer Ranger chirps a motherly warning to mama and her calf that they *really didn't want to come over here.* Big Mama did not appear the least bit thankful as she quickly scooted baby in the other direction, but we were thankful she had done so. Conversation resumed and we thought little of it until we spotted Mama, who has hidden her calf and circled back around to check us out. She is heading straight for us and she is looking none too friendly. We yell and hoot and she grudgingly backs off, only to come around again, looking decidedly more determined, head lowered and eyes red and glowing. The Devil Moose.

I had the immediate sense of what it must feel like to stand in front of an oncoming locomotive.

The river is at our backs, a Lodge Pole pine forest (which is noticeably bare of either hiding places or helpful limbs on which to climb) to the front — nothing upward but sky, and the ground is not cooperating in swallowing me up. I am feeling quite vulnerable — I never learned to shinny up a tree. Essentially, if Mama wants a piece of us, she has more than enough opportunity to go for it. I have heard how a moose will strike out with its front hooves, which can prove deadly. Third time around, we are all looking for a place to hide and this does not promise to be much fun. I take cover behind some fallen trees, and it looks like all hell is about to break loose. Mr. Volunteer Ranger appears to be contemplating one of those tall skinny pines, the rest have scattered.

Then (da da DAAAAA, *drum roll please*) the Star Wrangler comes along muttering and cussing about how he *doesn't have time for this CRAP*, grabs a shovel and KAwangs it against a rock. We are treated to the sight of Big Mama trotting off into the brush. Thankfully, she does not return, although I must admit, I kind of cottoned to the image of Mr. Volunteer Ranger, short and middle aged with little paunch, shinnying up that tree just once. Maybe next time.

OUTFITTER UPDATE

Along about half way through this project, I took the liberty of sending a few excerpts to my former employer, Chuck. It had been a number of years since we had spoken, at which time I had only made noise about writing these stories — thought maybe it would be best to check in and take a pulse. One never knows when you are going to offend, and Lord knows that was never the object here.

So I sent off four stories having to do with Darby Mountain Outfitters, one being "The Watermelon Crawl," which highlighted a few of Chuck's finer talents in particular, and then waited with baited breath. A month or so later, no letter bombs had arrived, no bounty was placed on my scalp, and not one load of buckshot was rumored to have flown my way from Wyoming. This I took to be a good sign.

Unbeknownst to me, Chuck was trying to reach me by phone. One day we finally did catch up and I was relieved to learn that he still had a sense of humor, and in fact had shared my stories at the annual employee Christmas dinner. Chuck went so far as to rehearse and then read each one aloud. This I also took to be a good sign. Apparently, the crew was so tickled with the stories that they wondered why I had not written about some of the other times they remembered as being notable. I assured him, there was more to follow. And of course, they wanted to make absolutely certain I wrote about the deer incident with Chuck's van... yes, I have dutifully included that as well.

Some topics I had not written yet might include a little diversion about Chuck and his particular affliction with varmints. Seemed they were always causing him grief one way or another. Sometimes he was at all out war with the pack rats who loved to raid camp if we stayed away too long. .. or the mystery rodents who loved to chew up the wires on only HIS van. If you want to get Chuck going, start him on the topic of rodents.

Then there is the time we were gassing up the truck prior to heading into the hills. Chuck pumped gas and I dutifully recorded the gallons and price. No sooner had we started down the road when the truck began to sputter and wheez. *(Aww Jeezuz, not the TRUCK!)* This was a potentially serious problem as we had guests on the way who expected to be packed into the mountains for their scheduled trip – this kind of operation runs on a tight schedule. Chuck barely got the rig off the road before it quit him, by which time he was winding up for a good fit of cussing. You may assume there was a fair bit of color to his cheeks.

Suddenly it dawned on him *("well for HEeeLL's sake…")* — he had only filled one of the two tanks, and then switched to the empty side before starting up. Chuck sheepishly switched back to the full tank, started the truck and headed back to the gas station in silence. As he was topping off the tank, I politely inquired of the mileage so as to complete the expense book? **"Shut UP"** he snapped! I just kind of sniggered and put the book away. Dang but those outfitters can get kind of uppity.

Another time, it was dusk at the Lake Alice camp and Chuck was setting to the nightly chore of horse wrangling. In the best of circumstances, he would hop on one of the horses bareback and head up the wooded trail to the pastures above, with the rest of the herd following passively behind. But this night a mare aptly named Stormy had other ideas, and Chuck soon found himself chasing the herd round and round the outside perimeter of our temporary corral (gaBOING gaBOING gaBOING). This was kind of comical if you did not happen to be Chuck. After a good chuckle I did take pity, and in my clumsy, flatlander way, helped to head the horses off from circling back again. Not, however, before a certain amount of colorful language was heard to escape the oft exemplary Mr. Thornton. If there had been any colorful language, it should have come from ME, since I tripped on the rocky terrain and landed flat on my face. Embarrassed, I squealed on Chuck instead. Without doubt I broke some kind of mortal cowboy code, though I tried not to do it again.

The last tell all I promised not to tell was the time when a group of women won a pack trip through some raffle to benefit The Rocky Mountain Elk Foundation — which was not all that newsworthy except they were a wild sort of women hell bent on riding topless the entire 13-mile trail out. Granted, this happened before my time, but I heard stories about it, and even saw some pictures. Until now, I thought I would be getting somebody in trouble by mentioning it. But Chuck's partner (that John Fellow) assures me he has gotten in all the trouble you could imagine, and then some. Well okay – a little hot water never hurt anybody.

It was a treat visiting with Chuck and we both had a good laugh. The only small glitch was that Chuck's brother Ivan had not yet received a proper reading of his chapter. Chuck admitted that he had tried to coax Ivan into coming to the company dinner for a proper "roasting," but Ivan was predisposed to some prior plans, possibly pursuing one of his three favorite things? Chuck says he cannot wait to see the look on Ivan's face and I am feeling rather fortunate to be well out of strangling distance whenever that event should happen. But Chuck told me not to feel too bad – like John Fellow said, there are few secrets in the mountains.

CHAPTER VI

Exploring The West

EXPLORING THE WEST

If you have ever fancied an outdoor adventure, the mountainous West is a very fine place to start. Montana, The Dakota's, Wyoming, Idaho, Utah, New Mexico, Nevada, or Arizona – there is something uniquely beautiful in all of them — I doubt you would be disappointed. Wyoming happens to be my personal favorite, so naturally I am biased. But there is a special place for everyone, so I encourage you to haul out the Atlas, pinpoint a few interesting places, call information and contact the local chamber of commerce. They will usually send an information packet if asked nicely. This is how I first got started back before I had ever been out West, much less heard of an outfitter. I wanted mostly to see some gorgeous country, and I did it by myself. Of course there are endless places to explore by car — but if you want serious backcountry, your best bet is an outfitter.

First order of business: Are you a flatlander? Do you think of "exercise" as pressing down on the accelerator while driving up a hill? Do you think of the "great outdoors" as the view out your patio window? And is your idea of "roughing it" a night of football without beer nuts? If so, an episode of Mutual of Omaha's Wild Kingdom might be enough adventure for you.

On the other hand, if the thought of a sunrise over a mountaintop; or waking up to the quiet sounds of a forest and of birdsong is inviting; and if you are not overly disturbed by the absence of indoor plumbing, then perhaps you are a good candidate for a wilderness pack trip.

TROUT IN FOIL

Can't very well send a person traipsing around the West without this staple method of cooking fish.

> trout
> green pepper
> onion
> salt & pepper
> lemon juice
> butter

Place trout on double-thick aluminum foil. Top with chopped green peppers and onions. Season with salt and pepper. Add a couple pats of butter and 2 tablespoons of lemon juice.

Fold foil securely around fish and place on grill. For a larger fish, total cooking time may be up to 30 minutes. Cook 15 minutes on each side. Smaller fish may take 9 – 13 minutes each side. Fish is done when flaky. Serve immediately as the fish will cool quickly.

If you are concerned about use of aluminum foil, as am I, use a preheated iron skillet with cover. Toxic levels of aluminum leach easily into foods and beverages from foil, cookware and canned soft drinks — bad news!

A Few Variations:

Try a few orange slices tucked into cavity of fish with lemon pepper and butter on the outside.

Thyme and dill also work fabulously with most fish. Substitute these spices for the green onion.

CAMPFIRE COOKING IN GENERAL

If you've a mind to undertake campfire cooking, here a few helpful hints.

First and most importantly, real campfire cooking is done over coals as opposed to actual flame — so just get that rousting bonfire image out of your head and save it for later when you are telling stories or burning the nightly garbage.

Once you have a decent fire going (don't be skimpy), add a quantity of wood pieces approximately 1 inch thick. Stack them like Lincoln Logs at least four to six deep, and let them burn to coals. Gather a good handful of wood chips or slivers, as once you get the fire perfect these will allow you to maintain it without causing high flames.

For grilling, rake out an even layer approximately 2 inch thick. Bank larger pieces off to the side and place grill frame approximately 6 inches above coals to cook steaks, etc., or to cook from frying pan or Dutch oven. If you have a good layer of coals you will have plenty of heat. In case of too much heat, thin out coal bed. If you notice an area of coals getting too low, slip a few chips in to boost it — just long enough to get dinner cooked and off the fire. Use a squirt bottle to temper flames that may flare up due to fat from grilling meat.

For eggs and pancakes, a lower temperature is necessary. Use a thinner bed of coals and make certain your griddle or skillet is preheated and maintained evenly. Then prepare yourself for some trial and error. This is the only way to learn, do not worry — every cook has to go through it, and it just may make a religious person out of you.

In the absence of handy grilling equipment, I have been known to place large rocks strategically in the coal bed, so that the base of my pan rests level upon them, thereby suspended. Modify coal bed thickness accordingly and do not use wet river rocks or granite, as they can explode.

A third option is to rig a tripod using three strong sticks or rods bound at the top, then suspend your pot at the appropriate height above the fire.

To cook directly on coals, make certain bed is no more than 1 inch thick. Too much heat will defeat the purpose, unless you have a hankering for char-food. Place Dutch oven directly on coals and cook as usual. This will require close monitoring until you become accustomed to this method. If top heat is needed and you happen to have a flat top Dutch oven, place a sparing layer of coals over the top. Here is where a lid-lifter comes in really handy. Otherwise, the hair on your knuckles will eventually grow back.

For pit cooking, dig a pit deep enough to submerge the Dutch oven, (6" or more) and wide enough to allow two inches space around it. Build your fire in the pit, or transfer coals from the main fire. Lay in an inch of coals on the bottom, set your Dutch oven in, bank sides with a thin layer of coals and add another thin layer on top of the oven. This is an excellent way to cook a whole turkey. I prefer to add several inches of water in the pot to steam the turkey and help keep if from burning. If the turkey is too tall for the Dutch oven, split it so that it will lay flatter. It is important that the cover be secure. An average sized turkey takes approximately two hours to cook, however you will need to monitor it until you get the knack.

If you are in the market for cooking gear, a Dutch oven with flat lid and raised lip is the best all around investment. With this you can cook stews, beans, meatloaves, breakfast, dessert, breads and whole turkeys — just about anything. A fold up grill frame is also an excellent addition, as is an enamel stock or coffee pot. Opt for the model that has the top metal handle (as opposed to small side handles), as this is best for retrieving your pot from hot coals. A good-sized cutting board is worth its weight in gold.

As a general rule, I prefer cast iron or enamelware as aluminum is poisonous and you do not want what comes of aluminum toxicity (Alzheimer's, immuno-deficiencies, etc.) Enamelware is best for heating liquids.

On the topic of campfires — without doubt, campfire cooking is a pleasing endeavor once you get your technique in place. There is nothing so mesmerizing and comforting as a lovely fire, but there is also nothing so dangerous. Fire should be used prudently, well away from trees or flammable materials. Strong windy days are definitely not advisable campfire days. Check local fire bans and conditions prior to undertaking a fire. Always keep a few gallons of emergency water nearby and make certain that you dowse that fire 100% before turning in for the night or departing your campsite. Retrieve non-burnable remains of trash (cans, glass, etc.) out of the fire and pack it out. In the case of fire bans, substitute a Coleman stove, which is clean to use and portable. In any event, my suggestions are not intended to replace either common sense or experience. Good judgment is always in season, and you must first depend upon your own.

COWBOY COFFEE

If you really want a taste of the West, and if you are not a'scared of hair sprouting on your chest, you must partake of this tradition. Bring your water to a rolling boil. Add appropriate quantity of coffee and a cup of cold water, then remove from fire. Grounds should sink to the bottom. Last one to drink from the pot gets an extra surprise. Enjoy!

AN EXCELLENT CAMP SECRET

One long-time camp cook secret is to rub a layer of liquid dish soap on the outside of enamelware before campfire use. This will help deter creosote from adhering to it, and make cleaning easier. This is the only place where I will use foil — as covering the outside of the pot with aluminum foil, in addition to the soap, is yet an easier way to maintain your enameled pots — in this case, the aluminum does not violate the contents.

WHAT IS AN OUTFITTER?

A very wise man once told me that the adventure begins when you get out of your car. He was right. However, the average flatlander has no business traipsing around the mountains alone. If you desire a wilderness vacation, then have no fear – there are people who get paid to do all the worrying. The worst you might contend with is saddle sores, flying pests and maybe some bad cooking. An outfitter is essentially the one with all the toys. He or she is the one to hire to pack you into the many beautiful backcountries.

If you fancy a hunting trip, then you are required by law to hire a guide in most any state where you are not a resident. Permitting, licensing and acquisition of tags varies from state to state.

Outfitters will pack you and your belongings, usually by horse and pack mule, four-wheel drive, or airplane, to some predetermined spot. There they will have set up camp and provided you with a dry place to sleep; hot, delicious (you hope) food, and with whatever guiding you have expressed interest in. During summer you may want to fish, sightsee, hike, ride horseback or go river rafting. This is a suitable time for families, couples, or just curious individuals hell bent for adventure. For the more aggressive types, you may be interested in a "progressive trip" which means traveling light and seeing lots. The entire camp moves every day or so, covering up to one hundred miles or more of gorgeous wilderness by horseback. The trip is tailored to your abilities, budget and interest. This also means your outfitter; cook and wranglers work doubly hard, so plan on a big tip. Be sure to bring lots of film and sunblock.

By fall, it is strictly business and if you are not out to hunt you should tread cautiously in the hills. Fall is when the hunters flock to the backcountry for a shot at some rugged hunting. Gone are the carefree deer and wild beasts meandering in the fields. They have headed for the pucker brush because they know — and they can smell it in the air. The whole mood of the forest changes, even the trees look different. Early September _is_ a good time to tour the mountainous highways by car, as the aspens are spectacular.

As for the controversy over hunting, I would first clarify that I am not a hunter. Secondly, I do not eat much meat. For anyone who might be sensitive on either of those issues, I might make the following points:

Where would you be if our ancestors had abstained from eating meat? Neither Daniel Boone, nor the American Indians would have gotten far eating grass, though the Indians, for certain would have faired better if Daniel had at least tried. Early settlers struggled to survive, as did the Native Americans for 10,000 years before them. (A tragedy, which I will avoid discussing here.) The hunter who braves the elements and all its challenges does a far fairer thing than the couch potato who waddles to the meat department to purchase a piece of old cow — which likely lived an inhumane life, followed by an inhumane death. A hunter has an opportunity to develop a respect for life — up close and personal as opposed to the dramatized images gained from television. In the wilds, you dance to the will of nature. Nothing is guaranteed (where integrity exists) and we will refrain from mentioning the other kind who manipulate the odds.

I watched many a hunter try his best and either succeed, or fail. Depending upon the hunter, I either empathized or hoped he learned a good lesson. No matter what, I learned a lot by placing myself in these environments, and though I chose not to hunt, I also chose not to judge those who did.

AND WHERE DO I FIND ONE?

In choosing an outfitter, it is best to ask many questions, and exercise caution. Do not be shy — not all outfitters are created equal. Ask for references and call them. Call several different outfitters and compare their services and fees. What are you expected to bring? Does the feller confess to having a weak spot for Jack Daniels, and has he been known, on more than several occasions, to crow at midnight? Does he sound shifty or mean? Alternatively, does he have about as much personality as a fencepost?

Outfitters are basically guys who love the hills and suffer the many headaches and losses of outfitting in order to be there. Not all of them possess the personality and skill to offer you a great experience, though some do it exceedingly well. Men with drinking problems have been known to call themselves outfitters and, of course, some are certifiably insane.

Any outfitter who is a member of the Rocky Mountain Elk Foundation will be listed in the back section of _Bugle_ magazine. Outfitters are located throughout the mountain states, Canada and various parts of the world. Call the ones that look interesting and be sure to ask for references. If questions make them squirm, hang up.

Bugle is generally available in the Western region of the US, but you may have difficulty finding a copy in the Eastern or more cosmopolitan areas. To contact _Bugle_ magazine directly, call 1-800-CALL-ELK, or visit their website at www.rmef.org.

For complete listings of outfitters from individual states, contact each state association directly to request a membership listing. Included in most outfitter listings are codes, which generally indicate what services and seasons they offer. From this you will also be able to pinpoint what region they operate from. There is a huge difference between East and West Montana, for instance. Do you prefer grasslands to mountains, desert to high alpine? Beyond that, you will have to trust your internal radar once you reach them by phone. If the gut says YES, ask more questions. If it says NO, hang up. If they happen to ask, in a roundabout way, if you can cook, DEFINITELY hang up!

STATE OUTFITTER ASSOCIATIONS

ALASKA PROFESSIONAL HUNTERS ASSOCIATION, Box 91932, Anchorage, Alaska 99509. (907) 522-3221

ALBERTA PROFESSIONAL OUTFITTERS SOCIETY, 6030 88th Street, Edmonton, Alberta T6C 4N6. (780) 414-0249 www.apos.ab.ca

COLORADO OUTFITTERS ASSOCIATION, PO Box 1949, Rifle, Colorado 81650. (970) 878-4043.

GUIDES OUTFITTERS ASSOCIATION OF BRITISH COLUMBIA, Suite 250, 7580 River Rd., Richmond, BC V6X 1X6. (604) 278-2688. Fax (604) 278-3440.

IDAHO OUTFITTERS & GUIDES ASSOCIATION, Box 95, Boise, Idaho 83701. (208) 342-1919.

MONTANA OUTFITTERS & GUIDES ASSOCIATION, Box 1248, Helena, Montana 59604. (406) 449-3578.

NEW MEXICO COUNSEL OF OUTFITTERS & GUIDES, INC.,
John Boretsky, Box 93186, Albuquerque, New Mexico 87199-3186.
(505) 822-9845.

OREGON GUIDES & PACKERS ASSOCIATION, Box 673, Springfield,
Oregon 97477. (800) 747-9552, Fax (541) 937-2819

WASHINGTON OUTFITTERS & GUIDES ASSOCIATION, 110 West 6th
Ave., Suite 398, Ellensburgh, Washington 98926. (509) 962-4222.

YUKON OUTFITTERS ASSOCIATION, Box 4548, Whitehorse, YT
Y1A 2R8. (403) 668-4118.

WYOMING OUTFITTERS ASSOCIATION, Box 2284, Cody, Wyoming
82414. (307) 527-7453.

YUKON OUTFITTERS ASSOCIATION, Box 4548, Whitehorse, Yukon Territory Y1A 2R8. (403) 668-4118

When you do find a good outfitter, it will be well worth the effort you invest
in doing so. You are in for an extraordinary experience, which may well change
your perspective on life as well as your appreciation for indoor plumbing.

Of my own experiences, I was fortunate enough to pick outfits fairly well.
The defining aspect of each experience was ultimately the personalities involved. A fish rots from the head down, meaning yet again – pick your outfitter wisely.

I narrowly escaped becoming employed by the all time outfitter from hell
one season – and only because his wife was tired of his fooling around with
female cooks (after all, that was how she met him herself) – luckily Mrs.
Outfitter insisted on a male cook and I was not offered the job. As it happened, I became marginally acquainted with the poor sot who did get the job
– he was both cook and wrangler in an outfit that should have had several

more hands. The boss had a penchant for impressive big mules, which were squirrelly to handle at best. And, the boss had an even greater penchant for booze, which made the crew decidedly squirrelly. They would get stuck in the outback for days on end with the boss on one of his binges, by which time they all wore the look of ones who have been through a war. I heard that cook finally cracked – started serving salad and Chinese noodles for breakfast and then quit. The boss, meanwhile, made a couple well-calculated trips over to our camp to check me out – seeing as I was one of the only women working that area... I made myself scarce until he finally got the message and quit coming around.

TICK & FLY SPRAY

For a variety of backcountry pests, try this homemade spray, which does not contain aerosols to pollute the environment, nor chemicals to contaminate the ground or <u>you</u>. Animals and people don't mind getting sprayed and it smells good. And besides, it is reputed to be very effective.

For the rampant outfitter variety of pests — I suggest Bullshit Repellent or maybe a good sledge hammer.

2 C.	white vinegar
1 C.	Avon Skin-So-Soft bath oil
1 C.	water
1 T.	eucalyptus oil (avail. at drug & health food stores)

CHAPTER VII

Epilogue: Lessons That Linger In The Heart

SUMMER OF 2000

As I have mentioned, my first dose of the West was well after the childhood years. During those travels I encountered many interesting people who reminisced of similar tales — they had all been dragged out West in their family's station wagon, and though they may have complained at the time, (as children do) they remembered this wild country most fondly — often returning with their own children years later.

I have no children of my own, but I do have a willing guinea pig by way of a young nephew... so it seemed fitting, as Brian was approaching the age of nine, to share the West with him. We planned a year in advance for a five-day pack trip in July of 2000 with Darby Mountain Outfitters, followed by five more days of camping and wandering around Wyoming, assuming I could then pry him away from Chuck. This would be Brian's first solo travel as he would have to fly from Maine to Salt Lake City, Utah. His mother's only stipulation was that I book a direct flight, that I never leave him alone. My only stipulation was that Brian receive ten horseback riding lessons timed up to the point of departure, along with $100 dollars of "mad money" for him to spend as he chose. In the meantime, I spent half the year worrying over potential disasters and hoping that all would go smoothly – right down to the last minute when his plane was due to land. Lord what if he missed it?

Luckily, my special buddy appeared and we headed straight for Wyoming. Brian chose dinner at a Chinese restaurant that night, and allowed as how he would like a nice hotel room in which to enjoy a hot shower and some TV time. Boy – did he have a lot to learn!

Of our 10 days together, Brian saw the inside of a hotel room only once. And while he might have felt deprived that first night, I figured he had the whole rest of his life for the watching the boob tube – this was our special time. Once he was in Chuck's world there was little chance of being bored with so much gorgeous country to see and new wonders to explore. Meanwhile, I had not laid eyes on Chuck since 1994 – six years of a <u>lot</u> of living. I barely slept that night thinking of all that had happened in those years – for certain, I was not the same girl who had driven away back then.

The following day we waited at the Poker Creek trailhead for Chuck, who had arranged to rendezvous within a certain window of time to pack us into Lake Alice. I forgot how "outfitter time" varies in reality from "normal" time. We ended up with hours to kill – nothing but us and the flies. I promised Brian they really were coming, as the hot summer sun passed slowly downward. We amused ourselves following moose trails through the alders, hunting small fish in the creek, spotting hawks and scouting for eagles — all the while waiting on pins and needles. Finally Brian curled up on his duffel and I kept watch for Chuck. It was getting late and soon we would set up camp for the night, turning our hopes toward tomorrow. A young bull moose wandered out of the trees and made his way down to the willows. I wondered if I had arranged more than my nephew could handle – starting with the 13-mile horseback ride from Poker Creek into Lake Alice?

But I have concluded that fear is something we cultivate as adults. Brian possessed a fair bit of confidence and along with his horseback riding lessons — seemed to have little fear. Even riding down steep rocky slopes that had you nearly standing in your stirrups did not seem to bother Brian, or if it did he never let on. Soon Chuck and the Gang was high on Brian's list – and he was fairly certain that he never wanted to leave. In the five days of Lake Alice, I believe he put nearly 60 miles of riding on his skinny behind. Brian never once fell off, got scared, or let that big old Palomino Toby get the best of him, though Toby is one of the world's most persistent lawn mowers. I got the feeling Toby knew his job very well, as he treated Brian like precious cargo for the duration.

At Lake Alice, Brian learned to fish and caught his very first trout. Cheryl (present day "Cookie") graciously taught him to cook his fish over the coals, which he later shared. Brian became an expert reel caster within days, carefully listening to every pointer that Rick and the other guys shared with him, meticulously duplicating each technique. Soon he could not wait to get down to the lake after dinner to fish, and only the promise of the evening fire (and the constant threat of the Booger Man) could lure him back to camp.

Lake Alice is a natural slide lake loaded with Bonneville Cutthroat Trout —a variety found exclusively in Lake Alice. Its water is deep aqua in color, and cold enough to make you feel alive – if it don't kill you first. I can recall swimming in that lake often, though the hot Southwestern summer has since spoiled my blood somewhat. Cheryl was a local gal and she didn't mind it a bit.. It seemed awfully funny to me, sitting around while someone else did the cooking – but I was determined to get used to it. I have since concluded that this is the best way to experience outfitting – as a guest.

At Lake Alice, my nephew learned to chop wood under the careful guidance of Rick, the camp wrangler that year. Brian had begged me for days to teach him, though he might have lost a few toes under my tutelage. I am sure he will never forget Rick's kind favor. Rick was one of Chuck's first and long-time summer guests who returned this season as an employee. There is nothing like a good chunk of time in the mountains on Chuck's Fitness Program to either discard the life you have created, or go running back to it. The most likely outcome would be to make some modifications to suit the person you have become. I would not dare to guess how the rest of Rick's summer went because wrangling is a tough job – but I do know that he made a lasting impression on Brian, who says he will remember Rick most.

At Lake Alice, my nephew stalked and trapped his first Golden Mantle Chipmunk. This came about one day when Chuck figured the boy needed something to amuse himself. No one would have guessed how diligently Brian would lay in wait nearly all afternoon, but you could see how badly he wanted to prove to Chuck that he could do it. Finally Brian got his prize. If only I had a video camera to capture the moment as he perched excitedly upon the box laughing in the sun. The chipmunk, however, was not impressed and quickly dug himself an escape under the lip of the box, taking off in a puff of dust. I have never seen a chipmunk move so fast.

One evening, Brian was fussing with the chairs around the campfire, when one good old boy growled, *"Why don't you jus' leave those chairs alone... there's more than e'nuff chairs around this fire... an' your little **pin ass** wouldn't cover one of 'em."* I heard just enough to turn around and see Brian with his mouth hanging open, not quite sure how to respond. I chirped *"Hey BRIAN — you over there learnin' new words for your BUHTT?"* He giggled and said, *"Yup,"* and the episode was over. We were blessed with a number of characters in camp that week. Besides Pete & Fred, the two seasoned ole boys who kept us all in stitches, we were in the company of six 19-year old boys on their post-graduation trip. Naturally, Brian and I soon had an agreement about what kind of talk got repeated at home, and the kind that stayed <u>right</u> <u>there</u> at the fire. Auntie would sure have a lot of explaining to do if kiddo got himself in trouble by repeating some colorful expletive, or perchance demonstrating how to light a fart. Sometimes, I thought I would never get the boy away from the evening fires.

Then came the day I had been waiting for — the ride to Mount Isabel. Lake Alice is nestled in the Commissary Mountain range, steeped by high foothills leading to higher mountains. The one place that has remained most treasured in my memory is that view from Mount Isabel where the Grand Tetons are visible to the naked eye over 100 miles away. I have often wished that I could be drop packed and stay up there for a week or so, just to absorb the place and do some landscape painting.

We headed up the mountain on a gloriously sunny morning, riding through groves of Quaking Aspen, shimmering in the breeze; forests of aromatic Lodge

Pole pine, pristine and still; traversing broad alpine fields of every imaginable wildflower with the smell of wild mint as the horses' hooves crushed it in passing. We came upon lightning trees and negotiated steep shale slopes where there was nothing between you and the bottom but hope and gravity. We rode upon densely compacted snowfields – the last of the season, and paused only briefly at the old sheepherder's campsite, which was empty. The first of July is too early for tending sheep on the mountaintop. July is, however, a fabulous time to enjoy Wyoming at its most lush and colorful state. By August, things have dried out considerably with fire bans often in effect and smoke from distant forest fires muddying up the skies.

At the summit of Mount Isabel (10,300 ft. el.) we perched on a lookout and traded Jolly Rancher jokes. Rick and Brian drifted off to share lunch and a nice talk about life. Later, Chuck took us on a little *impromptu* elk-spotting expedition down the mountainside. At that elevation, you can assume that walking down is a helluvalot easier than hiking up, so it wasn't long before the bright young Turks decided to "stay on the elk tracks" and let Chuck bring their horses down to meet them. I wonder if their whole lives will be as convenient to them as that one moment? Kind of young to give up climbing the mountain... Anyway, us "old timers" puffed back to the top, gathered the horses and headed down.

Perhaps the pinnacle of that ride was the moment when Brian got his horse Toby to canter. I will always remember him laughing like that. This too I wish I had on film. I should mention that "the hanging tree," icon for years and years on Mount Isabel, finally fell down, so there will be no more pictures – only memories.

Brian learned to name a lot of what he saw in those days, and we recorded it in his journal – along with a bright red Indian Paintbrush, Wild Lilacs, and Columbine pressed between the pages. This is God's classroom, and there is no sitting on hard chairs turning to stone, and there are no written tests. It is an experience of the senses where you learn by feeling, seeing, and hearing. Lessons that linger in the heart. Years from now, I wonder what pieces will remain in Brian's memory, and what will be forgotten? Brian never wanted to leave Lake Alice. As much as he might have enjoyed the following five days of wandering through Northwestern Wyoming with Auntie, he must have been aching to nuzzle up to Toby with some treats, or laugh with the guys by the fire, or just bask in the warmth of their attention. What nine-year old doesn't dream of hanging out with a bunch of good-natured guys who take you neat places and show you a new world? Besides, I am not nearly as amusing as a camp full of 19-year olds.

But one cannot stay in paradise forever — and according to the laws of nature, paradise never remains the same. It was inevitable that we would leave though we tried to make the days of Lake Alice last. Each and every bag would be packed and the good times tucked away. Brian and I would say our goodbyes and wander off with our memories while Chuck, Cheryl and Rick prepared to head full swing into their summer and fall season. Our little trip was something akin to a pebble on a mountain compared to all the work that lay ahead of them. Still, it was the precious highpoint of the year for me and I suspect Brian felt the same. Years ago, I remember being in another paradise, long before my travels West — a beautiful island off the coast of Maine. September sun warming my shoulders as I wrote and made paintings of the ocean and of the seaweed rising in the tide. I wondered then if I could hold that feeling and would it come back to me when I was far away? Later I was surprised at the potency of that feeling with just a quiet moment to think back on it. I learned something then, and now as I savored every moment of that last ride out I knew very well that I would return to Lake Alice just as easily in my thoughts. Memories are like that.

As I write this paragraph months later (October) Chuck is still at work, closing in on his last two weeks of hunt season. Probably pulling himself together for another rough day on the mountain where the snow is already thick. No doubt he is planning the big end of the season pack out in his mind and hoping that Mother Nature will cooperate.

As I write this paragraph, my extended family gathers for a Sunday potluck, because I am home to visit, because I will not be home at Christmas. The topic of Wyoming comes up and I tell them about our trip. I may have quipped about "Rocky Mountain Oysters" which is a Western tradition that my family knows nothing of. Brian overhears and pipes up that HE knows what they are

—— he saw them being served at Lake Alice, and besides his Daddy told him later. For just a moment I hold my breath, waiting for Brian to spill the undisguised truth that Auntie exposed him to fried bull balls.

Finally someone asks Brian to explain, and he responds.... *"They come out of the lake, and I'm not sure what they are, but I'm not eating them!"* Auntie is saved.

Someday I will tell Brian about this and many other things, but not just now. For the moment, it is good for him to be nine years old. For the moment, I am content to let it be so. And it is good to leave some things undiscovered so that we may find reason to return to paradise.

ROCKY MOUNTAIN OYSTERS

And now – the pinnacle of all recipes contained in this book. In fact, the crowning glory with which to end this ode to wandering and nonsense.

For my fellow Easterners, this may take some explaining – these "oysters" come from a special place, and I am not talking about the deep blue sea. In a land built on the back of cattle ranching, "Rocky Mountain Oysters" are as much a delicacy to cowboys as sea urchins and shark fins are to the Orient. It makes no difference that this particular delicacy formerly hung between the legs of a young bull species — a place where few Easterners would think to reach and pluck a snack. But the greater percent of young bulls are destined to become young geldings, meaning only the chosen get to keep their balls. Make a note of that… perhaps humans should emulate this practice? Anyways, as Jeffrey Dalmer might have excitedly inquired of Loreena Bobbitt, "You goin' eat dat?"

Near Missoula, Montana, there is a yearly celebration based on just this practice. They call it "The Testicle Festival," proudly touted on a huge billboard outside of town where they invite you to come and "have a ball" — pun most certainly intended. I have never attended the Testicle Festival, but I would, given the chance and I have often fantasized of ordering a plate of "oysters" for a visiting friend, only to fess up once they have swallowed, of what they have eaten. And yes, I have partaken of this delight – it tastes like most anything else that you might care to pound flat and fry within an inch of its existence. It might as well have been beef tongue or processed chicken patties for all I could tell, though I did wonder if there was any danger of sprouting chest hairs for several hours after. I did not. As to where to acquire fresh bull balls – you are on your own. As to how to cook them – I humbly offer the following.

BEER BATTER

1 C.	flour
1/2 tsp.	salt
1/2 tsp.	baking powder
1/2 tsp.	white pepper
1	egg
1 T.	oil
	beer (to desired thickness)

Mix dry ingredients, add egg and oil and blend well. Add enough beer to make a thick batter. Do not over stir.

Slice Rocky Mountain Oysters nearly in half so they lay out like a patty. Wash and pat dry. Preheat vegetable oil. Coat with Beer Batter and fry until golden brown.

An egg batter with crumbs also works nicely.

Recently, I attended a cattle branding at a local ranch where a friend and I had volunteered to cook for the cowboys for the day. A local character was in charge of the Rocky Mountain Oysters, and there was a bucket of the things in their natural state right beside me. I asked him *"well, what's happening next?"* He said he didn't know. *"Well... aren't YOU the one with all the balls?,"* I quipped. Seems to me a fella ought to have all the answers in that case.

ABOUT THE AUTHOR

Deborah Lynne Carlton is a native Mainer from a long line of Mainers. She attended first business college, then a Fine Arts college majoring in Silversmithing, minoring in Painting, and was a freelance painter for several years until a recession in Maine caused her to return to work as a legal secretary. This shift eventually led to a life re-evaluation after computer work began causing serious (though not permanent) deterioration to her eyesight. With never a prior thought of leaving Maine, she soon became overwhelmed with the desire to paint the great outdoors. Wide open plains, elusive rivers, red rock canyons and indigo mountains became her subjects as she left home for the first time in 1993 to begin a journey of remote and scenic destinations that continues to this day.

Artist Photo by Jerry Zielke © 1999

ISBN 155212748-6

9 781552 127483